(From the original front cover flap)

T0144669

MEDAL OF HONOR:
Historical Facts and Figures

In this book, Ron Owens has thoroughly researched all recipients of the Medal of Honor since its inception.

This book takes a new perspective on the Medal of Honor, examining the historical facts and figures of its recipients. It provides a top level view of this group in its entirety. With this new perspective, it analyzes and summarizes the historical facts in stunning detail.

Who are the men (and one woman) who have received America's highest award for combat valor? For the lucky ones who lived to wear it, what happened to them afterwards? Thanks to Hollywood, many could name Audie Murphy, Sergeant York, Douglas MacArthur and maybe a few others. But who are the more than 3,450 others?

While these stories are technically "trivia," they are not trivial. Read about:

•the boy who earned his Medal at the age of 12 and may have been 11 when his heroic acts were performed.

•the man who applied for his Medal only after seeing his name listed in an encyclopedia 23 years later.

•the man whose Medal is still listed under the wrong name because of the barrier caused by his native language Pawnee.

•the Medal recipient who was later assassinated by his own men.

•the sailor who earned his Medal of Honor in the Spanish-American War, 69 years before his nephew earned same award in Vietnam.

•the Marine who refused to wear his Medal in protest of another, more famous man's award which was not earned in combat.

•the recipient who was killed robbing a liquor store three years after his heroism.

… and many others. Success stories about generals, admirals, congressmen, millionaires and college presidents are intertwined with the more tragic, dysfunctional stories of recipients who became alcoholics, criminals, war protesters and committed suicide.

They were only human beings with all the strengths and weaknesses that demands. But once, they were heroes.

MEDAL OF
HONOR:

Historical Facts & Figures

Turner Publishing Company
Nashville, Tennessee

Other Books by the Author

Jelly Bryce: Legendary Lawman

Oklahoma Heroes

Oklahoma Justice

MEDAL OF
HONOR:

Historical Facts & Figures

By Ron Owens

Turner®
PUBLISHING COMPANY

www.turnerpublishing.com

Copyright © 2004 Ron Owens
Publishing Rights: Turner Publishing Company

No part of this book may be reproduced or transmitted in any form or
by any means, electronic or mechanical, including photocopying,
recording, or by any information storage and retrieval system,
without permission in writing from the publisher and/or author.

Turner Publishing Company Staff:
Darla Parrish, Editor
Ina F. Morse, Designer

Library of Congress Control No. 2004110567

ISBN 978-1-68162-240-8

Limited Edition

0 9 8 7 6 5 4 3 2 1

CONTENTS

PREFACE

The word "triumph" is derived from the Latin word *triumphus*. It was a grand parade and the highest honor that the emperor and citizens of ancient Rome could bestow upon a victorious general.

Sensitive to both the appearance and the realistic possibilities of a military *coup*, the Roman Senate required the returning general and his legions to wait outside the city limits while the Senate met to pass an ordinance to allow such an honor. Some generals remained camped at the city gates for several years before they received the honor...and some never did.

When they were allowed to enter, the grand day-long procession passed through streets festooned with garlands and strewn with flowers, lined with citizens cheering *Io triumphe*. Led by the Senators and magistrates, they were followed by the chained prisoners of war and the spoils of the conquered peoples. Their general in a gilded chariot drawn by four white horses preceded the conquering legions. Wearing a golden crown and carrying an ivory scepter, he was dressed in the purple and gold robes of Jupiter, their primary god. It was all symbolic that the conquering warrior was all of Rome's god even if only for a day. As the general rode through the cheering throngs, behind him stood a slave holding a laurel wreath over his head. This was but half of his duty. The other half was to periodically whisper in the general's ear "Remember, thou art only a man", a reminder that all glory is temporary. Some of history's figures seem to have known instinctively that while true as a generality, that is not one of the eternal verities.

The Medal of Honor is this nation's highest military award for valor in combat. The first two types, for the Army and Navy, are embossed with the head of Minerva, the Roman goddess of war. The Air Force Medal of Honor, created almost a century after the originals, displays the head of the Statue of Liberty. This book recounts some interesting facts about some of the men (and one woman) who have received this honor.

These vignettes relate the occurrences of heroism that occupied hours, minutes or sometimes mere seconds of the lives of

Medal of Honor recipients. But behind each name is an entire person and an entire life. A complete book could be written about each of the 3,440 individuals that have received this award. Our scope must be much more limited.

In a Utopian world, one would like to think ones nations' greatest heroes all went on to become generals, admirals, successful businessmen, statesmen, civic leaders or outstanding role models. Many, probably most, do meet these standards. But this, unfortunately, is not Utopia.

Some of these interesting facts are negative in nature. Some of these men became criminals, some became personal, professional and/or social failures, some took their own lives or the lives of innocent others. This brief exposition is not the proper forum for a discussion of shell shock, combat fatigue, post-traumatic stress disorder or any of the psychological trauma that have afflicted combat veterans. That is not to deny the existence of those phenomena. Neither is it reasonable to assume this is a recent phenomenon. These have doubtlessly afflicted men since they first took up arms against their own kind. On the contrary, the fact that these negative facts involve so few of the whole makes the majority all the more remarkable and all the more deserving of our admiration.

So, when dealing with something as fallible as human beings, it is important not to judge the whole by the sum of its parts, especially a distinct minority.

Because they were only men.

But once they were heroes.

How many of us can say as much?

FOREWORD
THE INCREASING PRICE OF COURAGE

Over the 140-odd years of its existence, the price of the Medal of Honor keeps rising, if a word like "price" can realistically be applied to things like blood, human life, self-sacrifice and valor. Overall, 614 of the 3,459 awards have been posthumous; slightly over 17 percent, but those figures are grossly misleading.

When the Medal was created in the Civil War, barely two percent of the awards were posthumous. The same was true of the Indian Campaigns. In fact, in the half century between the beginning of the Civil War and the beginning of World War I, 2,625 Medals of Honor were awarded and only 49 of them were posthumous. Even considering that over a third of those Medals were eventually rescinded, that is a telling figure.

From World War I to the present, 985 awards have been made and 558 were posthumous, over 56 percent.

From World War II to the present, 843 Medals of Honor have been awarded and 519 have been posthumous, over 61 percent.

From the Korean War to the present, 380 have been awarded and 252 have been posthumous, over 66 percent.

In the first half-century of its existence, over 98 percent of Medal of Honor recipients lived to receive and wear their Medals.

In the last half century, a recipient has less than one chance in three of living to wear his Medal.

As of November of 2003, there were 132 living Medal of Honor recipients in a nation of over 286 million people and it will probably be even fewer before this volume is printed. This is the lowest number of living recipients in over a century.

The phrase "one in a million" doesn't even begin to describe these men...and I'm not talking about numbers.

NUMBER OF LIVING MEDAL OF HONOR RECIPIENTS

September 1974—293
June 1985—254
January 1998—168
March 1999—158

June 2000—154
July 2001—150
April 2002—145
November 2003—132

METHODOLOGY

Each conflict or interim period between conflicts is covered in separate sections in chronological order similar to that of official U.S. Government publications chronicling the awards of the Medal of Honor. Within each section, the following format is used:

1. **TOTALS**-Each section is headed by a format showing the total number of Medal of Honor awards, the total number of recipients and the number of new recipients to account for multiple Medal recipients, and the total number of posthumous awards within each branch of service.

2. **PLACE OF BIRTH**-The total number of recipients by place of their birth is listed in the Civil War section because it was especially relevant in that conflict when most of the Army consisted of militia or volunteer units raised in the individual states. A total accounting for all conflicts is included at the end of the book.

3. **BY RANK**-A list of recipients by rank within each service branch with the number of posthumous awards in parentheses next to each rank. No number in parentheses following the number in a particular rank indicates that none of the awards in that rank were posthumous. Since many Medal recipients were promoted between the time of their action and their award, the numbers for the ranks are calculated by the rank held at the time of the action for which the Medal was awarded.

4. **POSTHUMOUS AWARDS**-Posthumous awards are calculated according to whether the recipient died before the award was made, whether from wounds, in combat action or from natural causes. A special section on Posthumous Awards is included in the Civil War section to explain discrepancies in those numbers.

5. **BY LOCATION OF ACTION**-The country or state where the Medal of Honor action occurred, if known. This section is included in areas where the actions occurred in more than one country or

state. Many Navy and Marine actions occurred on ships at sea and many times the location is not listed. One award lists only a longitude and latitude. If the ship was in port, the country or state of the port is listed.

6. **BY HOME STATE OF UNIT**-This category is included in the Civil War section due to the fact that units of that war were primarily raised and named from individual state militias rather than a nationalized military.

7. **BY BATTLE**-The individual battles within each conflict that produced the most Medal of Honor awards.

8. **MOST DECORATED UNITS**-The individual units by Division, Regiment and/or Company (or in the Navy, by ship) within each service branch that had the most Medal of Honor recipients for that conflict.

9. **MINORITY RECIPIENTS**-Where the ethnicity of the recipients is known, tabulations are included for each Medal of Honor recipient of Hispanic, American Indian, Black, Jewish or Asia-Pacific American descent. These are included either for each conflict or interim period or by a total tabulation at the end of the book.

10. **BY AGE OF RECIPIENT**-Although the dates of birth of many Medal recipients are unknown, most are known. This category provides for each section an average age of Medal recipients at the time of their action, a listing of the number of recipients in each ten-year age bracket or, if below 20, each individual age. It includes the oldest and youngest recipient in each period. A table at the end of the book lists the last surviving recipient for each conflict or interim period.

11. **TIME SPAN BETWEEN ACTION AND AWARD**-This category is included within the Civil War section due to a large block of late awards. Individual awards that were delayed for significant lengths of time in other conflicts are discussed within those sections.

12. **CRITERIA FOR AWARDS**-This category is included in the Civil War section due to some criteria for awards that were unique to that conflict. Other criteria that arose in later conflicts are discussed within those sections.

13. **NOTABLE INDIVIDUALS**-Special facts and circumstances concerning selected Medal of Honor recipients are included within the relevant sections.

14. **END LISTS**-At the end of the book are tabulations for all foreign-born recipients and all recipients by rank, service, location, conflict and state accreditation. Also included are lists of the most recent awards and tabulations on name errors, places of burial and award presentations.

Significant Dates

December 21, 1861-After a bill was introduced by Senator James W. Grimes of Iowa, chairman of the Senate Naval Committee, Congress and President Lincoln authorized the production of 200 Medals of Honor for award to enlisted men of the Navy and Marine Corps. The Navy Medal could be awarded for both combat and non-combat heroism.

July 12, 1862-Following the introduction of a similar bill by Senator Henry Wilson of Massachusetts, Congress and President Lincoln authorized the production of 2,000 Medals of Honor for Army enlisted men. They were to be presented only for heroism in combat.

March 3, 1863-Congress amended their previous resolution to include Army officers but not for officers of the Navy and Marine Corps.

March 25, 1863-Secretary of War Edwin M. Stanton awarded the first six Army Medals of Honor to survivors of "The Great Locomotive Chase" in Washington, D.C.

April 3, 1863-Secretary Stanton awarded the first Navy Medals of Honor in Washington, D.C.

March 3, 1915-Congress authorized the Navy Medal of Honor for award to officers of the Navy, Marine Corps and Coast Guard.

April 27, 1916-Congress authorized Medal of Honor recipients to receive a special pension of $10 a month for life beginning at age 65 if they had been honorably discharged from the service.

June 3, 1916-Congress directed an investigation and review of the 2,625 Medals of Honor that had been awarded up to that time.

February 17, 1917-911 names were stricken from the list. Included were the 864 members of the 27th Maine Volunteer Infantry, 309 of whom had been awarded the Medal for volunteering for extended duty in the Civil War and the remainder of the regiment by clerical error. Also stricken were awards to William F. "Buffalo Bill" Cody, several other civilian scouts from the Indian Wars and Civil War Surgeon Mary Walker.

July 6, 1960-Congress authorized a separate Medal of Honor for the Air Force.

August 14, 1961-Congress approved raising the special pension for Medal of Honor recipients from $10 per month to $100 per month and made it payable at age 50 instead of age 65. They also removed the requirement that the recipient had been separated from the service.

October 13, 1964-Congress approved dropping the age limit to 40 for receiving the special pension for Medal of Honor recipients.

October 31, 1965-Congress eliminated the age requirement for payment of the special pension.

October 18, 1978-Congress raised the special pension for Medal of Honor recipients to $200 per month. It was later increased to $400 a month with no age limitations. Currently, Medal of Honor recipients are allotted a pension of $1,000 a month for life, free transportation world-wide on government aircraft on a space-available basis, the right to burial in Arlington National Cemetery and, if they qualify and quotas permit, admission for themselves or their children to U.S. military academies.

First

T HE FIRST ACTION FOR WHICH A MEDAL OF HONOR WAS AWARDED occurred on February 13-14, 1861, at Apache Pass, Arizona. U.S. Army Assistant Surgeon Bernard J.D. Irwin undertook a rescue mission to relieve troops besieged by Apaches under Cochise.

THE FIRST ACTION OF THE CIVIL WAR FOR WHICH A MEDAL OF HONOR WAS AWARDED was by Private Francis E. Brownell of the 11th New York Fire Zouaves on May 24, 1861. While the regiment was marching through Alexandria, Virginia, the regimental commander, Colonel Ellsworth, tore down a Confederate flag from a local inn and was shot to death by the inn's owner. Private Brownell killed the owner. The Medal was not awarded until 1877.

THE FIRST AWARD OF ANY MEDAL OF HONOR was an Army Medal awarded to Private Jacob Parrott of Company K, 33rd Ohio Infantry, on March 25, 1863, for his participation in "The Great Locomotive Chase" in April of 1862.

THE FIRST AWARD TO A PARATROOPER was to Corporal Paul B. Huff of the 509th Parachute Infantry Battalion for actions near Carano, Italy, on February 8, 1944. His was the first of 15 Medals awarded to paratroopers during World War II.

THE FIRST AWARD OF THE NAVY MEDAL OF HONOR was to Signal Quartermaster Robert Williams for heroism during the Yazoo River Expedition on December 23-27, 1862.

THE FIRST ACTION FOR WHICH THE NAVY MEDAL WAS AWARDED was by Boatswains Mate John Williams for the battle against Forts Beauregard and Walker on Hilton Head, South Carolina, on November 7, 1861.

THE FIRST AWARD TO A NAVY OFFICER was to Lieutenant Abraham DeSomer for his actions on board the U.S.S. *Utah* at Vera

Cruz, Mexico, on April 21-22, 1914. It was awarded on January 8, 1915.

THE FIRST ACTION FOR WHICH THE NAVY MEDAL WAS AWARDED TO AN OFFICER was by Lieutenant Richard Pearson Hobson for his actions at Santiago de Cuba on June 3, 1898. Naval officers would not be eligible for the Medal for another 17 years but the award was made retroactively and awarded on April 29, 1933, by President Franklin D. Roosevelt.

THE FIRST AWARD TO A SUBMARINER was to Torpedoman Second Class Henry Breault of the submarine *U-5* on October 28, 1923. When the boat collided with a steamship at sea and began sinking, Breault returned to the torpedo room to rescue a shipmate, thus trapping both of them in the sinking sub. They were rescued by divers 31 hours later.

THE FIRST AWARD TO A SUBMARINER FOR ACTION IN COMBAT was awarded posthumously to Commander Howard Walter Gilmore for actions as commander of the U.S.S. *Growler* between January 10-February 7, 1943. After ramming a Japanese gunboat on February 7, Gilmore was wounded and unable to get back in the sub. To save his ship and men, he ordered the sub to submerge while he was still topside.

THE FIRST AWARD TO AN AVIATOR was to Navy Ensign Charles Hazeltine Hammann for heroism while piloting a seaplane and rescuing a downed comrade on August 21, 1918.

THE FIRST AWARD TO A HELICOPTER PILOT was posthumously awarded to Navy Lieutenant j.g. John Kelvin Koelsch whose unarmed helicopter was shot down while trying to rescue a downed Marine aviator in North Korea on July 3, 1951. Captured after evading the enemy for nine days, Koelsch died while a POW.

THE FIRST AWARD TO A MARINE was to Corporal John F. Mackie for heroism on board the U.S.S. *Galena* in the attack on Fort Darling, Virginia, on May 15, 1862.

THE FIRST AWARD TO A MARINE OFFICER was to a group of officers (one Lieutenant Colonel, four Majors and four Captains) for actions at Vera Cruz, Mexico, on April 21-22, 1914. The awards were made in a group on December 4, 1915.

THE FIRST AWARD TO A BLACK MARINE was made posthumously to Private First Class James Anderson Jr. of 2nd Platoon, Company F, 2nd Battalion, 3rd Marines, 3rd Marine Division, for saving other Marines by throwing himself on a grenade in Vietnam on February 28, 1967.

THE FIRST AWARDS TO MARINE AVIATORS were to pilot Second Lieutenant Ralph Talbot and observer Gunnery Sergeant Robert Guy Robinson for aerial battles over Belgium on October 8 and October 14, 1918.

THE FIRST AWARD TO A MEMBER OF THE U.S. AIR FORCE (after it became a separate service on September 18, 1947) was posthumously awarded to Major Louis J. Sebille of the 18th Fighter-Bomber Group, 5th Air Force, for actions near Hanchang, Korea, on August 5, 1950.

THE FIRST AWARD OF THE NEWLY APPROVED AIR FORCE MEDAL OF HONOR was to Major Bernard Francis Fisher, 1st Air Commandos, for landing and rescuing a crashed comrade in Vietnam on March 10, 1966.

THE FIRST (and thus far only) AWARD TO A MEMBER OF THE U.S. COAST GUARD was posthumously awarded to Signalman First Class Douglas Albert Munro for heroism in evacuating a trapped battalion of Marines on Guadalcanal on September 27, 1942.

THE FIRST AWARD TO A BLACK SERVICEMAN was to escaped slave Robert Blake serving as "Contraband" on the gunboat *Marblehead* in the U.S. Navy on December 25, 1863, in the Stono River, South Carolina. His award was made by General Order 32 on April 16, 1864.

THE FIRST ACTION WHICH EARNED A MEDAL OF HONOR FOR A BLACK SERVICEMAN was by Sergeant William H. Carney of Company C, 54th Massachusetts Colored Infantry at Fort Wagner, South Carolina, on July 18, 1863. The award was made on May 23, 1900.

THE FIRST AWARD TO A BLACK OFFICER was to Army First Lieutenant Ruppert L. Sargent, Company B, 4th Battalion, 9th Infantry, 25th Infantry Division. Lt. Sargent was killed after throwing his body over two grenades to protect his men on March 15, 1967, in Vietnam.

THE FIRST ACTION BY A BLACK OFFICER to merit the award of a Medal of Honor was by Army Captain Charles L. Thomas of the 614th Tank Destroyer Battalion, 103rd Infantry Division, near Climbach, France, on December 14, 1944. Originally awarded the Distinguished Service Cross, Thomas survived the war but died in 1980. President Bill Clinton awarded his Medal posthumously on January 13, 1997.

THE HIGHEST-RANKING BLACK MEDAL OF HONOR RECIPIENT was Army Lieutenant Colonel Charles Calvin Rogers, 1st Battalion, 5th Artillery, 1st Infantry Division, for his actions in Vietnam on November 1, 1968. Rogers later retired from the Army at the rank of Major General.

THE FIRST AWARD TO A JEWISH SERVICEMAN was to a 17-year-old drummer boy, Private Benjamin Levy of Company B, 1st New York Infantry, for actions at Glendale, Virginia, on June 30, 1862. The award was made on March 1, 1865.

THE FIRST ACTION BY A JEWISH SERVICEMAN for which a Medal was awarded was by Private David Orbansky of Company B, 58th Ohio Infantry, for his gallantry at Shiloh and Vicksburg. Although his Medal was not awarded until August 2, 1879, Orbansky's actions at Shiloh occurred almost three months before Private Levy's battle at Glendale.

THE HIGHEST-RANKING JEWISH MEDAL RECIPIENT is Army Captain Jack H. Jacobs of Military Assistance Command, Vietnam, for his actions on March 9, 1968. Jacobs retired from the Army as a full Colonel.

THE FIRST AWARD TO AN AMERICAN INDIAN SERVICE-MAN was to Pawnee Scout Co-Rux-Te-Chod-Ish for his actions at Republican River, Kansas, on July 8, 1869. Pursuing an enemy Indian, he was accidentally shot by one of his own command. The Medal was presented on August 24 of that year.

THE FIRST AWARD TO AN AMERICAN INDIAN OFFICER was to Army Second Lieutenant Ernest Childers of the 45th Infantry Division for heroism near Oliveto, Italy, on September 22, 1943.

THE HIGHEST RANKING AMERICAN INDIAN MEDAL RECIPIENT is Navy Commander Ernest Edwin Evans. He was mortally wounded on October 25, 1944, in a naval battle near Samar in the Pacific Ocean while commanding the U.S.S. *Johnston*.

THE FIRST AWARD TO A HISPANIC SERVICEMAN was to Navy Seaman John Ortega for service aboard the U.S.S. *Saratoga*. Although his dates were not specified in the citation, the award was made on December 31, 1864.

THE FIRST AWARD TO A HISPANIC MARINE was to Private France Silva for his actions at Peking, China, between June 28-August 17, 1900, during the Boxer Rebellion.

THE FIRST AWARD TO A HISPANIC OFFICER was awarded posthumously to Marine First Lieutenant Baldomero Lopez of Company A, 1st Battalion, 5th Marines, 1st Marine Division, for absorbing the blast of a grenade to protect his comrades at Inchon, Korea, on September 15, 1950.

THE HIGHEST RANKING HISPANIC MEDAL OF HONOR RECIPIENTS were Army Captain Euripides Rubio, 1st Battalion, 28th Infantry, 1st Infantry Division, and Marine Captain M. Sando

Vargas Jr. for separate actions in Vietnam in 1966 and 1968, respectively. Rubio's award was posthumous while Vargas retired from the Marine Corps as a full Colonel.

THE FIRST ACTION AND THE FIRST AWARD TO AN ASIA-PACIFIC AMERICAN was to Army Private Jose B. Nisperos of the Philippine Scouts. He was severely wounded during a battle on Basilan Island during actions against Philippine outlaws on September 24, 1911. His left arm was broken and he received several spear wounds. Unable to stand, he continued firing his rifle with one hand keeping the party from being overrun.

Nisperos was the first Filipino to be awarded the Medal of Honor, the first Asia-Pacific recipient and the last one until World War II.

THE FIRST AWARD TO AN ASIA-PACIFIC AMERICAN OFFICER was made to Captain Francis B. Wai of the 34th Infantry Division for actions on Leyte, Philippine Islands, on October 20, 1944. The award was presented posthumously on June 21, 2000. Wai was also the highest ranking Asian-Pacific American to receive the award to that time.

THE FIRST AWARDS FOR A NON-COMBAT ACTION were to seven sailors, Lewis Horton, Luke Griswold, John Jones, Hugh Logan, George Moore, Charles H. Smith and Maurice Wagg. On the U.S.S. *Rhode Island* on December 30, 1862, they engaged in an attempt to rescue crewmen of the sinking U.S.S. *Monitor* off the coast of Cape Hatteras, North Carolina. Logan and Smith's awards were originally listed as two of the Navy's three posthumous awards in the Civil War but it was later shown that they survived.

THE FIRST AWARDS FOR ACTIONS OUTSIDE THE UNITED STATES AND ITS CONTIGUOUS WATERS were to 17 sailors of the U.S.S. *Kearsarge* for destroying the Confederate ship *Alabama* off the coast of Cherbourg, France, in the English Channel on June 19, 1864.

THE ONLY AWARD TO A WOMAN has been the Medal of Honor given to Dr. Mary E. Walker by President Andrew Johnson on November 11, 1865. Dr. Walker acted as a Contract Acting Assistant Surgeon in a series of battles from First Bull Run in 1861 to the Battle of Atlanta in 1864. She also spent four months as a Prisoner of War of the Confederates. Her award was rescinded in 1917 but restored in 1977.

THE OLDEST MEDAL RECIPIENT at the time of the action was General Douglas MacArthur who was 62 years old at the time of his evacuation from the Philippine Islands in early 1942.

THE YOUNGEST MEDAL RECIPIENT at the time of the action was Willie Johnston, a drummer boy with the 3rd Vermont Infantry. He received his Medal when he was 13 but his unspecified actions occurred during the Peninsular Campaign (March 17-August 2) and the Seven Days Battles (June 25-July 1) of 1862. Since he was born on an unspecified day in July of 1850, he was at most 12 and possibly 11 when he performed the actions for which he earned the Medal.

THE LONGEST DELAY in time between the action and award of the Medal of Honor was for Army Corporal Andrew Jackson Smith of the 55th Massachusetts Volunteer Infantry. A former slave, Smith saved the unit flag from capture during the battle of Honey Hill, South Carolina, on November 30, 1864. He was posthumously awarded the Medal of Honor on January 16, 2001, more than 136 years after his actions.

THE ONLY AWARD TO A PRESIDENT OF THE UNITED STATES was made on July 16, 2001, when Lt. Col. Theodore Roosevelt was posthumously awarded the Medal of Honor for his actions during the Spanish American War on July 1, 1898. (See Most Recent Awards)

THE CIVIL WAR
1861-1865

ARMY-1,198 awards to 1,197 individuals, 1,196 men and one woman. These include awards to one civilian scout, one civilian assistant surgeon and one double award for actions that occurred during the Civil War. Thirty (30) awards were posthumous.

NAVY-307 awards to 307 individuals including two (2) to civilian pilots (of ships, obviously, not aircraft). Two (2) awards were posthumous.

MARINE CORPS-17 awards to 17 individuals. None were posthumous.

TOTAL-1,522 awards to 1,521 individuals, 1,520 men and one woman. Awards include one civilian scout, one civilian assistant surgeon, two civilian pilots, one double award and 32 posthumous.

THE MELTING POT

In the true spirit of the diversity of America, of the 3,440 persons who have been awarded Medals of Honor, at least 746 of them were born in other countries, more than one-fifth. Others were born in American territories that later became part of the United States.

Over half of these 746 served in the Civil War. Over one-fourth of Medal of Honor recipients in the Civil War were born in another country. Even taking into account the probability that some were American children of American parents who happened to be living or traveling abroad, this is an overwhelming number to be involved in an adopted country's civil war.

BY PLACE OF BIRTH:

New York	285	Ireland	139
Pennsylvania	197	England	69

Ohio	135	Germany	65
Massachusetts	79	Canada	32
Maine	60	Scotland	22
Vermont	39	France	11
Michigan	32	Prussia	6
New Hampshire	34	Norway	7
Illinois	31	Sweden	5
Indiana	33	Wales	6
Connecticut	32	Holland	3
Maryland	29	Belgium	3
New Jersey	27	Denmark	2
Rhode Island	18	Hungary	2
West Virginia	18	Italy	2
Virginia	16	Russia	2
Kentucky	15	Spain	2
Delaware	9	Switzerland	2
District of Columbia	7	Austria	1
Tennessee	6	Chile	1
Iowa	4	Europe	1
Missouri	3	India	1
North Carolina	3	Malta	1
Wisconsin	3	Mexico	1
Alabama	2	At sea in the English Channel	
Mississippi	2	Aboard a U.S. ship	1
Louisiana	1		
Arkansas	1	**TOTAL**	**387**
Georgia	1		
California	1		
Indian Territory	1		
Texas	1		
Unknown	9		

TOTAL 1134

BY RANK:

ARMY		MARINE CORPS	
Major General	3	Sergeant	7
Brigadier General	9	Orderly Sgt.	3

Colonel	34 (1)	Corporal	5
Lieutenant Colonel	19	Private	2
Major	30		
Captain	88 (1)	**TOTAL**	17
First Lieutenant	90		
Second Lieutenant	29		
Lieutenant	9		
Chaplain	3		
Surgeon	3		
Assistant Surgeon	5		
Asst. Surg. (Civ.)	1		
Sergeant Major	18 (1)		
First Sergeant	50 (2)		
Commissary Sergeant	5		
Quartermaster Sgt.	4		
Color Sergeant	3 (1)		
Sergeant	209 (11)		
Corporal	158 (2)		
Private	401 (11)		
Principle Musician	1		
Musician	12		
Chief Bugler	4		
Bugler	2		
Drummer	3		
Blacksmith	1		
Farrier	1		
Saddler	1		
Civilian Scout	1		

TOTAL   1197 (30)

NAVY

Capt./Afterguard	4
Capt./Forecastle	16
Capt./Foretop	2
Capt./Hold	1
Capt./Maintop	2

Capt./Top	9
2nd Capt./Top	1
Chief Bos'ns Mate	3
Bos'n's Mate	28
Chief Quartermaster	3
Signal Quartermaster	5
Quartermaster	33
Coxswain	37
Landsman	32 (1)
Quartergunner	9 (1)
Fireman 1st Class	4
Fireman 2nd Class	3
Fireman	4
Master At Arms	3
Paymasters Steward	2
1/c Pilot	1
Pilot	2
Yoeman	2
Carpenters Mate	1
Gunners Mate	5
Sailmakers Mate	1
Armorer	1
Coal Heaver	10
Shell Man	1
Engineers Cook	1
Ships Cook	1
Seaman	53
Ordinary Seaman	23
Cabin Boy	1
2nd Class Boy	1
3rd Class Boy	1
Contraband	1
TOTAL	**307 (2)**

POSTHUMOUS AWARDS:

Originally, only 12 awards from the Civil War were officially noted as posthumous awards. Three were awarded to Navy men and nine to Army men in the following ranks:

ARMY		NAVY	
Captains	2	Captain of the Afterguard	1
Sergeants	3	Coxswain	1
Corporal	1	Quartergunner	1
Privates	3		

In their two-volume 1995 history of Medal recipients (see Bibliography), Lang, Collins and White were able to determine many dates of death and places of burial for Medal recipients. They were able to show that a Navy Coxswain and a Captain of the Afterguard did not die in their Medal-award actions but a Navy Quartergunner did and a Landsman died as a POW before he could receive his award.

They did not find any of the original nine posthumous Army recipients who survived but did find another 19 recipients whose awards were posthumous. Five had been killed in their award action, one died while a POW and 22 others died either in subsequent combat actions or of natural causes before they could receive their awards. Four enlisted men who were cited for their involvement in "The Great Locomotive Chase" were hanged as spies by the Confederates in Atlanta, Georgia, on June 18, 1862, prior to being awarded their Medals in September of 1863: Private Samuel Robertson, Co. G, 33rd Ohio Infantry, Sergeant Major Marion A. Ross, 2nd Ohio Infantry, Sergeant John Scott, Co. F, 21st Ohio Infantry, Private Samuel Slavens, Co. E, 33rd Ohio Infantry.

Three other men were hanged with them who, as civilians, were not considered to be eligible for the Medal. The highest-ranking posthumous award was to a Colonel who died less than a month before his Medal was awarded in 1893.

The last posthumous award was made on January 16, 2001, by President William J. Clinton to an Army Corporal, Andrew Jackson Smith, who had been considered and rejected in 1916. This award was made more than 136 years after the action.

MOST ARMY AWARDS BY HOME STATE OF UNIT:

New York	238
Pennsylvania	156
Ohio	134
Illinois	93
Massachusetts	66
Michigan	51
Indiana	43
Vermont	43
West Virginia	32
Missouri	30
Iowa	28
New Jersey	25
Maine	24
New Hampshire	21
Wisconsin	18
Minnesota	16
Rhode Island	16
Maryland	14

AWARDS BY LOCATION OF ACTION:

Virginia	676
Mississippi	152
North Carolina	124
Alabama	120
Tennessee	104
Georgia	85
Pennsylvania	63
Louisiana	57
South Carolina	35
Maryland	26
At Sea	18
Multiple states	16
Arkansas	12
Florida	8
Missouri	7
West Virginia	7
Kansas	4
Kentucky	3
Texas	3
Delaware	1
D.C.	1

Note: All the above awards listed as "At Sea" occurred in two naval actions—in the Atlantic Ocean (50 miles off of Cape Hatteras, North Carolina) and in the English Channel off of the Cherbourg Peninsula.

MOST AWARDS BY BATTLE:

Vicksburg, Miss.	125
Petersburg, Va.	108
Mobile Bay, Ala.	97
Fort Fisher, N.C.	70
Gettysburg, Pa.	61
Sailors Creek, Va.	60
Spotsylvania, Va.	40

MOST AWARDS BY ARMY REGIMENT:

1st New Jersey Cavalry	12
1st West Virginia Cavalry	11
83rd Indiana Infantry	10
2nd Minnesota Infantry	10
8th Missouri Infantry	10
21st Ohio Infantry	10
1st Rhode Island Lt. Artillery	9

Chapins Farm, Va.	33	29th Massachusetts Infantry	9
Chancellorsville, Va.	26	55th Illinois Infantry	9
Fredericksburg, Va.	24	61st Pennsylvania Infantry	8
The Wilderness, Va.	23	1st New York Cavalry	8
Cedar Creek, Va.	21	17th Michigan Infantry	8
Antietam, Md.	20	104th Illinois Infantry	8
(Some awards are for more		16th Illinois Infantry	8
than one battle.)		4th Iowa Cavalry	8

MOST AWARDS BY COMPANY:

Company H, 2nd Minnesota Infantry   8
Company D, 104th Illinois Infantry   7
Company G, 1st Rhode Island Lt. Artil   7
Company A, 3rd Indiana Cavalry   4
Company M, 2nd New York Cavalry   4

Numerous others with 2 or 3 winners.

NAVY/MARINE CORPS AWARDS:

The U.S. Navy and Marine Corps awarded 324 Medals of Honor for actions during the Civil War. Medals were awarded to men assigned to 75 separate ships. Almost half of the awards were made for participation in only two battles:

1. The battle of Mobile Bay, Alabama, on August 5, 1864. It was in this battle in which Admiral Farragut, tied high upon the mast of his flagship USS Hartford so he could see above the smoke of the battle, made his immortal quote "Damn the torpedoes, full speed ahead!" Ninety-seven (97) Medals of Honor were awarded to participants in this battle. The Navy awarded Medals to 89 sailors and 8 Marines on 8 ships for this battle alone. The most decorated ship was the U.S.S. *Richmond* that made awards to 27 sailors and 3 Marines. Three sailors on the *Richmond* were also cited for the battle of Port Hudson on March 14, 1863.

2. The series of battles for Fort Fisher, North Carolina, in December 1864 and January 1865. Seventy (70) Medals were awarded including 60 Navy Medals to 54 sailors and 6 Marines serving on 13 ships during those battles. The U.S.S. *Agawam* and U.S.S. *Ticonderoga* were awarded 10 each.

MOST AWARDS BY SHIP:

U.S.S. *Richmond*	33
U.S.S. *Brooklyn*	22
U.S.S. *Kearsarge*	17
U.S.S. *Hartford*	12
U.S.S. *Lackawanna*	12
U.S.S. *Agawam*	10
U.S.S. *Ticonderoga*	10

BLACK RECIPIENTS:

The Union Army contained numerous units of Colored Troops, segregated units with black enlisted men and white officers. During the Civil War, 25 black men were awarded Medals of Honor, 18 in the Army and 7 in the Navy. Thirteen (13) of the 18 Army awards were given for action on September 29, 1864, at Chapins Farm, Virginia. Four of the seven Navy awards were given for the assault on Fort Morgan on August 5, 1864.

AGE OF RECIPIENTS:

It has been said that war is a young man's endeavor, usually because of the physical and emotional stress involved. So it was with the Civil War but even more so. It was a war of many contradictions, not the least of which was 50-year-old privates led by 19-year-old colonels. It could almost have been called the teenager's war. Admittedly, many dates of birth from the first half of the 19th Century are inexact, records are sparse or non-existent and many dates are unknown. But of those that are known, it can be determined that at least 202 men received the Medal of Honor for actions in their teens or pre-teens in the Civil War. This is almost one-seventh of all the Medals awarded. The documented ones are in the following age groups:

Ages 50-59	10
Ages 40-49	39
Ages 30-39	226

Ages 20-29	970
Age 19	95
Age 18	41
Age 17	32
Age 16	20
Age 15	6
Age 14	5
Age 13	2
Age 12 or younger	1
Age Unknown	74
AVERAGE AGE:	25

YOUNGEST RECIPIENT:

The only pre-teenager known so far appears to be William "Willie" Johnston, a Musician in Company D of the 3rd Vermont Infantry. He was at most 12 and possibly 11 at the time of the actions for which he received his Medal at age 13. See his entry under Notable Individuals.

OLDEST RECIPIENT:

Navy Captain of the Forecastle Henry Shutes. Born in 1804, he received his Medal in 1866 (at age 62) for a series of actions beginning in 1862 (at age 58).

TIME SPAN BETWEEN ACTION AND AWARD:

It is reasonable to assume that a Medal of Honor would be awarded fairly promptly after the action for which it is awarded. By fairly promptly, one would assume that to mean within three to five years after the action. In fact, legislation enacted in 1918 says that recommendations for the Army Medal must be made within two years of the date of the deed and awarded within three years after the deed. A recommendation for the Navy Medal must be made within three years and awarded within five years. As we shall see, those limitations are not always met.

Of the 1,522 Medals of Honor awarded for action in the Civil War, only 683 were actually awarded during the war or within a few months after its end. The dates on 21 of the citations are unknown but 818 were awarded after the war, some long afterwards. In the quarter century after the war's end, Civil War Medals were awarded in the following numbers:

1866-1869	33
1870-1879	31
1880-1889	39

The United States Navy and Marine Corps were usually very prompt with their awards of the Medal with the notable exception of one Navy Quartermaster whose Medal wasn't awarded until 1916, more than 53 years after the action occurred.

It would appear that the Army was much tardier with their awards but that is deceptive. The fact is that most of the Army awards merely came much later. A contributory factor was that it was the only medal available. Corresponding with the twenty-fifth anniversary of the end of the war, a national resurgence of the Grand Army of the Republic (an organization for Union Army veterans) began in 1890. This resurgence and the resulting pressure on politicians brought the Congressional approval for the following number of awards of the Medal of Honor for Civil War actions during these years:

1890	22
1891	41
1892	66
1893	67
1894	127
1895	62
1896	88
1897	117
1898	64
1899	25
1900-17	39

The biggest block of awards, in the summer of 1894, was for the battle of Vicksburg in 1863. Within that group, a single block of 59 awards were for the "volunteer storming party." This is the largest group of awards for a single action. The date of one award is not known and another was made in 1884 but most of them were awarded during the last decade of the century.

On the morning of May 22, 1863, a group of 150 men were chosen to storm the fortress of Vicksburg, their mission to build a bridge across a ditch in front of the fort while under heavy fire. The bridge would then give access for a general assault by other troops.

Since none were expected to survive, it was decided to accept only volunteers and only unmarried men. Characterized by one author as "The Forlorn Hope", it was just that. The bridge was not built, the assault was unsuccessful and the volunteer storming party sustained at least 85 percent casualties.

The outstanding exception for a non-posthumous award is Henry Lewis. Henry was a 20-year-old corporal in Company B of the 47th Ohio Infantry Regiment when he volunteered to bring subsistence stores past the Confederate defenses at Vicksburg, Mississippi, on May 3, 1863. He was awarded the Medal of Honor for his actions almost 54 years later, on April 17, 1917, 13 days after the United States had entered World War I. He was 74 years old.

CRITERIA FOR AWARDS:

Many of the criteria for awards of the Medal of Honor during the Civil War were unique to that conflict and were not to be repeated in future conflicts. That uniqueness was perhaps due to the nature of the conflict, the only one (excepting the American Revolution) in which Americans were fighting Americans.

Wounds seemed to count for quite a bit and especially, because of the lack of sophisticated medical care, disfiguring wounds. These included:

32 posthumous awards.
167 had wounds mentioned in their citations.
7 who suffered "severe disability".
5 listed as "permanently disabled".
1 who lost an eye.
1 who lost both eyes.

22 who suffered amputated limbs including:

10 who lost a leg.

1 who lost both legs.

9 who lost an arm.

1 who lost both arms.

1 who lost a hand.

92 had it prominently mentioned in their citations that they captured prisoners.

96 served time as a POW.

Some awards were for no more than escaping or suffering harsh treatment and surviving places like Andersonville.

6 were mentioned for capturing Confederate general officers.

12 had their horses shot out from under them.

23 were message runners.

11 were ammunition runners.

136 were mentioned for rescuing comrades (or their dead bodies).

The primary motivator for awards in the Civil War would appear to have been The Grand Old Flag. Individual units carried not only a national standard (the Union Stars and Stripes) but a flag unique to that unit, often handmade by the wives and mothers of the soldiers. Besides being a visible symbol of the unit's *espirit de corps*, in the era before electronic communications the units used the flags as markers for rallying points or sending messages. Over one-third of all the Army Medals awarded, 467, were for either capturing a Confederate unit's flag, saving a Union flag from capture, planting the Union flag on some objective, recapturing a Union flag from the Confederates or some form of "gallantry as a color bearer."

NOTABLE INDIVIDUALS:

ADELBERT AMES-First Lieutenant Ames won his Medal of Honor at the first battle of Bull Run, Virginia, on July 21, 1861, while assigned to the 5th U.S. Artillery and only 14 months after graduating fifth in the West Point Class of 1861. Born on October 31, 1835, he later rose to the rank of Major General. He served as the post-war governor of Mississippi, in the U.S. Senate and later served in the Spanish-American War. He died on April 13, 1933, at the age of 97, the last surviving general officer of either side of the Civil War.

FRANK D. BALDWIN-Double Medal of Honor recipient. See under the Indian Campaigns.

ROBERT BLAKE-Blake, whose rank in the U.S. Navy is listed as "Contraband", was an escaped slave who performed heroically while serving on the U.S. Steam Gunboat *Marblehead* on the Stono River near Charleston, South Carolina, on Christmas Day of 1863. On April 16, 1864, he became the first black man to receive the Medal of Honor.

FRANCIS E. BROWNELL-On May 24, 1861, the first Union troops entered the state of Virginia as an occupying power. Colonel Elmer Ellsworth of the 11th New York Fire Zouaves saw a Confederate flag flying from the house of a man named Marshall in Alexandria. Ellsworth cut the flag down and was immediately shot to death by Marshall. Marshall was shot and killed by Private Brownell. Although his Medal of Honor was not awarded until January 26, 1877, this was the first Civil War deed to merit the award.

DANIEL BUTTERFIELD-Brigadier General Butterfield was awarded his Medal of Honor in 1892 for actions on May 4, 1863, at Salem Heights, Virginia. Before either of these events, Butterfield had composed the bugle call "Taps" at Harrison's Landing, Virginia, in the summer of 1862. As an example of the mournfully respectful tune's universal acceptance, less than ten months after it was composed, it was played at the funeral of Confederate General Stonewall Jackson. Later promoted to Major General, Butterfield died on July 17, 1901, and was buried at West Point.

WILLIAM H. CARNEY-Sergeant Carney of Company C, 54th Massachusetts Colored Infantry, performed heroically at the battle of Fort Wagner, South Carolina, on July 18, 1863. Although his

Medal of Honor was not awarded until May 23, 1900, this was the first action by a black man to merit the award.

EUGENE A. CARR-Colonel Carr of the 3rd Illinois Cavalry received his Medal of Honor for actions at Pea Ridge, Arkansas, on March 7, 1862. He ended the war as a Major General and later became a renowned Indian fighter. Dying on December 2, 1910, he was buried at West Point.

JOSHUA L. CHAMBERLAIN-Colonel Chamberlain received his Medal of Honor for leading his 20th Maine Infantry in a bayonet charge on Little Round Top at Gettysburg on July 2, 1863. Chamberlain participated in 24 engagements during the war, was wounded six times, ended the war as a Major General and personally received the formal surrender of Lee's Army of Northern Virginia. After the war, he was elected Governor of Maine for four terms and served 13 years as President of Bowdoin College. He died on February 24, 1914, at the age of 85.

NEWTON MARTIN CURTIS-Brigadier General Curtis was cited for his actions at Fort Fisher, North Carolina, on January 15, 1865, where he was the first Federal soldier inside the works. He ended the war as a Major General and later became a Treasury Agent, a New York State Assemblyman and a U.S. Representative. He died on January 8, 1910.

THOMAS W. CUSTER-The younger brother of the more flamboyant George Armstrong Custer, 2nd Lieutenant Tom Custer became the Army's only recipient of two Medals of Honor during the Civil War and the first recipient of two Medals. He received them for actions three days apart during the first week of April, 1865, at Namozine Church and Sailors Creek, Virginia. Both awards were for capturing Confederate battle flags.

Tom Custer was killed on June 25, 1876, while serving as a Captain under his brother George at the Little Big Horn River. When his body was found, he had been scalped, his skull was crushed flat, his stomach and heart were torn out and he had a dozen arrows in him. The body had to be identified by a tattoo on his arm. A

Sioux warrior named Rain-in-the-Face, who had vowed to eat Tom Custer's heart after being arrested by him the year before, allegedly claimed to have eaten part of Custer's heart. This legend is generally discounted because cannibalism was as repulsive to Indians as it was to whites. But the heart <u>was</u> cut out.

JAMES DUNLAVY-Private Dunlavy was cited for capturing Confederate General Marmaduke at Osage, Kansas, on October 25, 1864. After Dunlavy fired at the General and missed, Marmaduke's nearsightedness caused him to approach Dunlavy to berate him, thinking he was a Confederate soldier. He wasn't.

RICHARD ENDERLIN-Enderlin was a Musician in Company B of the 73rd Ohio Volunteer Infantry. On the first two days of the battle of Gettysurg in July of 1863, Enderlin voluntarily armed himself and took part in the fighting. During the battle, Enderlin saw one of his comrades wounded but the man was too close to the Confederate lines to be rescued. That night, spurred on by the man's cries for water, Enderlin crawled out to the wounded man's position and brought him into the Union lines on his back. The trip took nearly two hours.

The man Enderlin rescued, 43-year-old Private George Nixon, died from his wounds several days later but one of his great grandsons, Richard M. Nixon, later became the 37th President of the United States.

JOSEPH L. FOLLETT-Sergeant Follett enlisted at the age of 18 in 1861. The next year, he was cited for his actions at New Madrid, Missouri, in Company G of the 1st Missouri Light Artillery and later received the Medal of Honor. Commissioned as an officer, at 19 he became the youngest officer in the Union Army in command of a battery of artillery. He eventually rose to Lieutenant Colonel.

MANNING F. FORCE-Brigadier General Force was cited for his Medal of Honor at Atlanta on July 22, 1864, and later became a Major General. A Harvard law graduate and Judge, he died on May 8, 1899, at the age of 74.

LEWIS A. GRANT-Colonel Grant received his Medal of Honor for actions at Salem Heights, Virginia, on May 3, 1864. Later becoming a Major General, he served as Assistant Secretary of War from 1890-1893. He died on March 20, 1918, at the age of 90.

JOHN F. HARTRANFT-Colonel Hartranft received his Medal of Honor for actions at the first battle of Bull Run on July 20, 1861. Eventually becoming a Major General, he was the special provost marshal for the trial of President Lincoln's assassins. After the war, he later served two terms as Governor of Pennsylvania. He died on October 17, 1889, at the age of 58.

FRANCIS J. HERRON-Lieutenant Colonel Herron of the 9th Iowa Infantry was cited for actions at Pea Ridge, Arkansas, on May 7, 1862. He was appointed a Major General on November 29, 1862, at age 25 the youngest two-star general on either side. After the war, he became a U.S. Marshal and served as Secretary of State for Louisiana. He died on January 8, 1902, at the age of 64.

OLIVER O. HOWARD-Brigadier General Howard lost an arm in his Medal of Honor action at Fair Oaks, Virginia, on June 1, 1862. Promoted to Major General, he later commanded forces against the Apache chief Geronimo in Arizona, established Howard University in Washington, D.C., and served as Superintendent of West Point. He died on October 26, 1909, at the age of 78.

ORION P. HOWE-Howe was long thought to be the youngest recipient of a Medal of Honor but was eventually supplanted by Willie Johnston (see next entry). Howe was a drummer boy with Company C of the 55th Illinois Infantry. He was severely wounded while taking a message to General Sherman requesting more ammunition during the battle of Vicksburg. His citation states he was 14 years old but he was born on December 29, 1849, and the date of action was May 19, 1863, making him only 13 at the time of his heroism. He received his Medal at the age of 46 in 1896 and died at the age of 80 in 1930.

WILLIE JOHNSTON-Serving as a Musician in Company D of the 3rd Vermont Infantry, Johnston was and remains the youngest

Medal of Honor recipient. Although his exact birthdate is not known, it was in July of 1850. He was cited for gallantry during the Seven Days and Peninsular Campaigns of March-August, 1862. Therefore, when he performed the actions for which he received the Medal of Honor, he was at most 12 and possibly even 11 years old! He received his Medal in September of 1863, two months after his 13th birthday.

JOHN LAFFERTY (LAVERTY)-Navy Fireman John Laverty (his true name) was belatedly discovered to be a previously unknown double recipient of the Medal of Honor. He earned his first award under the name John Lafferty on May 25, 1864, while serving on the U.S.S. *Wyalusing* in the Roanoke River of North Carolina. His second award under his true name of Laverty was earned on September 14, 1881, while serving on the U.S.S. *Alaska* in Callao Bay, Peru.

His first citation indicates he was born in 1842 in New York City while the second shows his birth in June of 1845 in County Tyrone, Ireland. In the 17 years between awards, his rank advanced from Fireman to First Class Fireman.

It was not until the research conducted by Lang, Collins and White (see bibliography) showed that both Lafferty and Laverty had died in Philadelphia on November 13, 1903, were buried in Mount Moriah Cemetery in Philadelphia, and were in fact the same man.

ARTHUR MacARTHUR Jr.-First Lieutenant MacArthur of the 24th Wisconsin Infantry received his Medal of Honor in 1890 for his actions at Missionary Ridge, Tennessee, in 1863 at the age of 18. He carried the regimental flag up the ridge after several other color bearers were killed. In 1912, then-General MacArthur was giving a speech at a reunion of his regiment when he collapsed and died of a stroke. His adjutant wrapped his body in the same flag he carried up Missionary Ridge and then suffered a fatal stroke himself.

MacArthur would pass on his military heritage. His eldest son, Arthur III, would earn a Navy Cross, Distinguished Service Medal and the captaincy of a battleship. Fifty-two years after his award, in

1942, another son, General Douglas MacArthur received the Medal of Honor for his defense of the Philippines in World War II. This was the first of only two instances of a father and son both receiving the Medal.

JOHN F. MACKIE-Corporal Mackie was cited for actions on board the U.S.S. *Galena* in the attack on Fort Darling, Virginia, on May 15, 1862. His was the first Medal of Honor awarded to a member of the U.S. Marine Corps.

NELSON A. MILES-As a 23-year-old Colonel of the 61st New York Infantry, Miles was cited for his actions at Chancellorsville in May of 1863. In this battle he received one of four wounds he sustained during the Civil War. Remaining in the Army, he received the surrender of the Apache chief Geronimo during the Indian Campaigns. He retired as a Lieutenant General and died on May 15, 1925.

GEORGE W. MINDIL-As an 18-year old Captain in Company I of the 61st Pennsylvania Infantry, Mindil was cited for his actions at Williamsburg, Virginia, in May of 1862. He was promoted to Colonel at the age of 19.

LLEWELLYN P. NORTON-Sergeant Norton was cited for heroism at Sailors Creek, Virginia, on April 6, 1865. He was promoted to Sergeant Major and breveted to First Lieutenant. Norton was awarded the Medal of Honor on July 3, 1865, but had already mustered out of the service and couldn't be found. Twenty-three years later, Norton saw his name in a list of Medal of Honor recipients in Appleton's Cyclopedia. After contacting the War Department, he received his Medal in May of 1888.

JACOB PARROTT-As an 18-year-old Private in Company K, 33rd Ohio Infantry, in April of 1862 Parrott was one of the volunteers on the mission to hijack a railroad train 200 miles behind Confederate lines in Georgia that later became known as "The Great Locomotive Chase". The 19 soldiers and 5 civilians, all in civilian clothes, were captured and 8 were court-martialed and hanged in

Atlanta as spies. Six of the men were paroled and on March 25, 1863, received the first six Medals of Honor in Washington, D.C., from Secretary of War Edwin Stanton. The youngest of the group, Private Jacob Parrott received the first Medal of Honor ever awarded.

GALUSHA PENNYPACKER-Enlisting at 16 and a Captain at 17, as a Colonel in the 97th Pennsylvania Infantry on January 15, 1865, Pennypacker was cited for heroism at Fort Fisher, North Carolina. Although he didn't receive his Medal of Honor until 1891, Pennypacker was promoted to Brigadier General a month before his 21st birthday, making him the only general officer in the history of the U.S. Army who wasn't old enough to vote for the President who appointed him. He died in Philadelphia on October 1, 1916, at the age of 72.

PETER RAFFERTY-Private Rafferty of Company B, 69th New York Infantry, was cited for his bravery at Malvern Hill, Virginia, on July 1, 1862. Only 17 years old at the time, he was wounded 7 times in 7 days, re-enlisted in 1864 and rose to the rank of Captain.

JOHN C. ROBINSON-Brigadier General Robinson lost his left leg as a result of his actions at Laurel Hill, Virginia, on May 8, 1864. He advanced to Major General and later served as the Lieutenant Governor of New York. He received his Medal of Honor three years before he died on February 18, 1897, two months before his 80th birthday.

WILSON SMITH-Corporal Smith of Battery H, 3rd New York Light Artillery, was cited for his heroism on September 6, 1862, at Washington, North Carolina. As a result of his wounds, one of his legs was amputated the next day, on his 21st birthday.

JOHN W. SPRAGUE-Colonel Sprague of the 63rd Ohio Infantry gained his Medal of Honor for actions on July 22, 1862, at Decatur, Georgia. Promoted to Major General, he later became one of the founders of Tacoma, Washington, and was buried there when he died on December 24, 1893, at the age of 76.

WAGER SWAYNE-Lieutenant Colonel Swayne of the 43rd Ohio Infantry earned his Medal of Honor at Corinth, Mississippi, on October 4, 1862. The son of U.S. Supreme Court Justice Noah Haynes Swayne, he lost his right leg in battle on February 2, 1865. He died on December 18, 1902.

ALLEN THOMPSON-JAMES THOMPSON-Brothers Allen and James Thompson received their Medals of Honor for actions at White Oak Road, Virginia, on April 1, 1865. At that time, Allen was 17 years old and James was only 15.

MARY E. WALKER-Born in 1832, Dr. Mary E. Walker served as a Contract Acting Assistant Surgeon from 1861 to 1864, treating wounded and ill soldiers in battles from the First Battle of Bull Run in 1861 to the Battle of Atlanta in 1864. She also spent four months as a Prisoner of War of the Confederates in 1864. President Andrew Johnson awarded her the Medal on November 11, 1865, making her the only female recipient.

Dr. Walker's Medal was one of those rescinded by the review board in 1917 but she refused to turn in her Medal and stubbornly continued to wear it until her death in 1919. This action was later reconsidered and, on June 10, 1977, President Jimmy Carter restored the award.

FRANCIS E. WARREN-Corporal Warren of Company C, 49th Massachusetts Infantry, earned his Medal of Honor at Port Hudson, Louisiana, on May 27, 1863. He later became the first Governor of Wyoming. Warren Air Force Base in Cheyenne, Wyoming, is named for him.

ORLANDO B. WILLCOX-Colonel Willcox of the 1st Michigan Infantry was cited for heroism at the first battle of Bull Run on July 20, 1861. Later promoted to Major General, he served in Arizona during the Apache wars and the town of Willcox, Arizona, was named for him. He died on May 10, 1907, at the age of 84.

JOHN WILLIAMS-Navy Captain of the Maintop John Williams performed the first action for which the Navy Medal of Honor was awarded while serving on the U.S.S. *Pawnee* in the attack upon Mathias Point on June 26, 1861. Although his was the first naval action, he was not awarded the first Navy Medal (see Robert Williams).

ROBERT WILLIAMS-Seaman Robert Williams was the first member of the U.S. Navy to be presented the Navy Medal of Honor for his actions on the U.S.S. *Commodore Perry* in the attack upon Franklin, Virginia, on October 3, 1862. Although his action was 16 months after that of John Williams, Robert Williams' Medal was presented in April of 1863 while John's wasn't awarded until July of that year.

SAMUEL C. WRIGHT-Private Wright of Company E, 29th Massachusetts Infantry, received his Medal of Honor for actions at Antietam on the bloodiest single day of the Civil War, September 17, 1862, when both sides suffered over 38,000 casualties. Wright, 19, would go on to forge a war record few men could match. He fought in 30 battles, was wounded five times, lost his right eye, was reported dead twice and received two battlefield promotions.

NON-COMBAT ACTIONS
1865-1871

ARMY-1 award to 1 individual. Not posthumous.

NAVY-12 awards to 12 individuals, 10 of whom were new recipients and 2 awards to double Medal recipients, both of whom earned their first Medal during the Civil War. None were posthumous.

TOTAL-13 awards to 13 individuals, 11 of whom were new recipients and 2 awards to double Medal recipients, both of whom earned their first Medal during the Civil War. None were posthumous.

During the interim periods between significant conflicts, both the Army and Navy continued to award Medals of Honor; the Navy due to their tradition of honoring non-combat heroism and the Army in what was to become a less-frequent tradition of honoring long and faithful service.

The single Army award during this period was to a Sergeant Major in the Army Engineers for his service during 1839-1871.

Of the dozen Navy awards, nine (9) were for saving shipmates from drowning. Three awards were given for the single act of saving two men from the U.S.S. *Winooski* off the coast of Eastport, Maine, on May 10, 1866. The remaining three awards were for actions during a fire, saving a ship and assisting after the wreck of another ship.

Some chroniclers place two of these awards, the second awards of two Navy men who earned their first Medals during the Civil War, within that statistics for that conflict. I have chosen not to for three reasons: Both first Medals were for combat actions while the second Medals are not; the generally accepted date for the end of the Civil War is April 9, 1865, when General Robert E. Lee surrendered. While minor combat actions and the surrender of large numbers of Confederate troops occurred for more than two months following that date, that date still reflects the end of major resistance; if further justification is needed, perhaps the best is the rationale that the ending date for a war is better determined by when the soldiers think it's over than when the politicians sign a piece of paper saying so. The 1901 book *Deeds of Valor* states that on March

31, 1865, the Union Army had a strength of 980,086 troops. Thirty-one days later, following Lee's surrender, their strength was 100,516.

Almost one-fourth of the Medal recipients in the Civil War were foreign-born. The Navy men exceeded that figure during this period. Only two of the dozen were American born, one each from Pennsylvania and Massachusetts. The birthplace of a third with an apparent Anglican name is unknown. The others were born in Wales, England, Denmark, Norway, Cuba and four from Ireland.

BY RANK:

NAVY:		ARMY:	
Capt./Afterguard	2	Sergeant Major	1
Capt./Hold	1		
Coxswain	1		
Seaman	5		
Quartermaster	1		
Boatswain's Mate	1		
Apprentice	1		

AWARDS BY SHIP:		AWARDS BY LOCATION:	
U.S.S. *Winooski*	3	At sea off Eastport, Maine	3
U.S.S. *Don*	1	At sea off New London, CT	1
U.S.S. *Huron*	1	At sea off Virginia	1
U.S.S. *Rhode Island*	1	At sea off Pensacola, FL	1
U.S.S. *Sabine*	1	At sea off New Orleans, LA	1
U.S.S. *Saginaw*	1	At sea in Cape Haiten, Haiti	1
U.S.S. *Tallapoosa*	1	At sea in New York harbor	1
U.S.S. *Yucca*	1	Sandwich Islands (Hawaii)	1

AGE OF RECIPIENTS:

50-59	2
40-49	0
30-39	2
20-29	7
16 or 17	1
Unknown	1

AVERAGE AGE:	30

YOUNGEST RECIPIENT:

Navy Apprentice Frank Du Moulin, born on an unspecified date in 1850 received his Medal for saving a shipmate from drowning on September 5, 1867, when he would have been 16 or 17 years of age.

OLDEST RECIPIENT:

Army Sergeant Major Frederick William Gerber was born on an unspecified date in 1813 and received his Medal for his career spanning 1839-1871. He was either 57 or 58 at that time.

NOTABLE INDIVIDUALS:

JOHN COOPER-Coxswain Cooper became the Navy's first recipient of two Medals of Honor. Born John L. Mather on July 28, 1832, he was already a 19-year veteran sailor when he earned the first Medal at Mobile Bay, Alabama, on August 5, 1864. He earned his second Medal on April 26, 1865, again at Mobile but this time for rescuing a comrade during a fire. He was discharged in 1866 and died in New York on August 22, 1891.

PATRICK MULLEN-Navy Boatswain's Mate Mullen was the Navy's second recipient of two Medals of Honor. His first Medal was earned for manning his cannon under fire at Mattox Creek, Virginia, on board the U.S.S. *Wyandank* on March 17, 1865. The second was earned aboard the U.S.S. *Don* off the coast of Virginia on May 1, 1865, when he saved an officer from drowning.

INDIAN CAMPAIGNS
1861-1898

ARMY-426 awards were presented to 424 individuals. Of the 424, 423 were new recipients. Five Medals were given to double Medal recipients: one award was the second award to an individual who earned his first Medal during the Civil War and four awards were to two double-Medal recipients whose actions all occurred during the Indian Campaigns. Thirteen (13) awards were posthumous.

The U.S. Army conducted numerous campaigns against American Indians between 1861 and 1898. In fact, the first action for which a Medal of Honor was awarded occurred during the Indian Campaigns (see Bernard J.D. Irwin under Notable Individuals). Given the vast distances and mobility involved in the western United States, naturally the cavalry carried the brunt of the action. That fact is borne out by the following statistics.

Although the Army conducted many campaigns and skirmishes against many separate tribes of Indians, it is obvious from the following statistics that the fiercest and most frequent fighting occurred against the Apaches in Arizona/New Mexico and Sioux in Montana and the Dakotas.

BY RANK:

MAJOR	2	
CAPTAIN	10	
1ST LT.	18	
2ND LT.	12	
CONTRACT SURGEON	1	
ASSISTANT SURGEON	2	
SGT. MAJOR	1	
1ST SGT.	35	(1)
SGT.	94	(3)
CORPORAL	54	(4)
PFC	1	
PRIVATE	154	(5)
MUSICIAN	3	

INDIAN SCOUT	6
FARRIER	6
BUGLER	4
TRUMPETER	4
HOSPITAL STEWARD	1
BLACKSMITH	7
WAGONER	2
SADDLER	3
CIVILIAN SCOUT	2
CIVILIAN GUIDE	2
TOTAL	424* (13)

*One individual, Frank Baldwin, earned his first award during the Civil War at the rank of Captain. He earned his second award during the Indian Campaigns at the rank of 1st Lieutenant.

BY LOCATION OF ACTION*

Arizona	153
Montana	89
Texas	66
South Dakota	30
New Mexico	18
Nebraska	14
Colorado	12
Kansas	12
Idaho	5
Wyoming	4
Mexico	3
California	2
Idaho/Montana	2
Indian Territory	1
Kansas/Colorado	1
Minnesota	1
Utah	1
Not stated	12 **
TOTAL	426*

BY SPECIFIC BATTLE

Chiricahua Mntns (1869)	32
Cedar Creek, MT (1876-77)	31
Little Big Horn, MT (1876)	24
Apache Campaign (1872-73)	21
Wounded Knee, SD (1890)	19
TOTAL	127

(Over one-fourth of the Medals awarded were for these five campaigns)

*Awards to 424 individuals and two double awards.

**Although the location of these award actions is not specifically stated, 9 of them were awarded for actions against the Apache in the Winter of 1872-73 [and therefore may be assumed to have occurred in Arizona, New Mexico or Mexico] and 3 were for actions against the Sioux.

MOST DECORATED UNITS:

BY REGIMENT:		BY COMPANY:	
8th Cavalry	90	Co. B, 8th Cavalry	34
6th Cavalry	50	Co. G, 1st Cavalry	18
5th Infantry	46	Co. H, 6th Cavalry	16
7th Cavalry	45	Co. L, 8th Cavalry	15
1st Cavalry	32	Co. G, 8th Cavalry	13
5th Cavalry	31	Co. F, 5th Cavalry	10
4th Cavalry	24	Co. B, 7th Cavalry	9
3rd Cavalry	21	Co. I, 9th Infantry	9
2nd Cavalry	15	Co. I, 7th Infantry	8
9th Cavalry	15	Co. D, 7th Cavalry	8
7th Infantry	8	Co. E, 8th Cavalry	8
23rd Infantry	4	Co. F, 8th Cavalry	8
24th Infantry	3	Co. C, 5th Infantry	8
10th Cavalry	3		

AWARDS BY TYPE OF UNIT:

Cavalry units	326
Infantry units	68
Artillery units	5
Hospital Corps	1
Signal Corps	1
Indian Scouts	17
Pawnee Scouts	1
Not listed unit or unknown	5
TOTAL	**424**

BLACK RECIPIENTS:

The heritage of the Colored Troops of the Civil War, segregated units with all black enlisted men and all white officers, was continued in the renowned "Buffalo Soldiers", the 9th and 10th Cavalry and the 24th and 25th Infantry. Eighteen (18) black men, all enlisted men in these units, received Medals of Honor during the Indian Campaigns.

AGE OF RECIPIENTS:

50-59	3
40-49	26
30-39	109
20-29	267
Age 19	2
Age 18	1
Age 17	2
Age 16	1
Unknown	13

AVERAGE AGE: 28

YOUNGEST RECIPIENT:

Born February 26, 1858, Private Frederick Berendahl of the 4th U.S. Cavalry was 16 years old when he earned a Medal of Honor on December 8, 1874, at Staked Plains, Texas.

OLDEST RECIPIENT:

As rapid as promotions sometimes were during the Civil War, they were sometimes equally slow in the post-war Army. Born on May 12, 1822, First Lieutenant Robert McDonald of the 5th U.S. Infantry was 54 years old when he earned his Medal of Honor at Wolf Mountain, Montana, on January 8, 1877. Even at that, the Medal wasn't presented to him until 1894 when he was 72, seven years before his death in 1901.

NOTABLE INDIVIDUALS:

FRANK D. BALDWIN-Captain Baldwin became the Army's third double Medal of Honor recipient and the first one to earn them in separate wars. He earned his first Medal of Honor for leading a charge of his men of Company D, 19th Michigan Infantry, at Peach Tree Creek, Georgia, on July 12, 1864. Born on June 26, 1842, he later served in the Indian Wars against the Kiowa, Apache, Cheyenne, Arapaho and Sioux. He earned a second Medal of Honor at McClellans Creek, Texas, on November 8, 1874, for rescuing two white girls who had been kidnapped by Indians. He later served in the Spanish-American War and commanded the 4th Infantry in the Philippines in 1900. He retired as a Brigadier General in 1906 (at the then-mandatory retirement age of 64) and died on April 22, 1923. He was buried in Arlington National Cemetery.

OSCAR R. BURKARD-Private Burkard of the Army Hospital Corps earned his Medal of Honor during an uprising of Chippewa Indians on Lake Leech, Minnesota, on October 5, 1898. His was the last Medal of Honor earned in an Indian Campaign.

CO-RUX-TE-CHOD-ISH (MAD BEAR)-This man, a Sergeant in the Pawnee Scouts, was the first American Indian awarded the Medal of Honor. It was awarded on August 24, 1869, for an action at the Republican River in Kansas and has two oddities. First, he was wounded by one of his own troops while in pursuit of another Indian. Second, the Medal was awarded to the right man but the wrong name was recorded because of the language barrier. His true name was Co-Tux-A-Kah-Wadde (Traveling Bear). The error, while understandable, has never been corrected.

Eleven other American Indians serving as Scouts were awarded Medals during the Indian Campaigns, ten of them *en masse* on April 12, 1875, for a campaign against the Apaches in Arizona. Again representative of the language barrier, one of them is listed under the shortest name (obviously not his true name) for any Medal of Honor recipient—"Jim".

HENRY HOGAN-Hogan, First Sergeant of Company G of the 5th

Infantry, earned two Medals of Honor in less than a year, one against the Sioux and one against the Nez Perce. An Irish immigrant, he retired from the Army in 1879 after 15 years of service. He was the last Army man to earn two Medals of Honor. His second Medal was earned for saving the life of his severely wounded Lieutenant, Henry Romeyn, at Bear Paw Mountain, Montana, on September 30, 1877. Lt. Romeyn earned his own Medal of Honor that day and this is the second known instance in which a man earned a Medal for saving another Medal recipient.

BERNARD J.D. IRWIN-Assistant Surgeon Irwin performed the first action for which an Army Medal of Honor was awarded. At Apache Pass, Arizona, on February 13-14, 1861 (two months before the Civil War began), Irwin rescued an infantry unit trapped by Apaches under Cochise. Although his Medal was not awarded until 1894, this is chronologically the first of all Medal of Honor actions.

EMANUEL STANCE-Sergeant Stance, of Company F of the 9th Cavalry, was the first black man to earn the Medal of Honor during the Indian Campaigns. He earned it on May 20, 1870, at Kickapoo Springs, Texas. While later serving as a First Sergeant in Nebraska, he was killed by his own men in December of 1887.

AUGUSTUS WALLEY-Private Walley, a black man in Company I of the 9th Cavalry, received his Medal of Honor for action against Apaches in New Mexico on August 16, 1881. He served 30 years in the Army and was recommended for a second Medal of Honor for saving a wounded Major's life in the Spanish-American War but it was down-graded to a Certificate of Merit* (see note at the end of this section). At the beginning of World War I, he was recalled to active duty at the age of 60, promoted to First Sergeant and placed in charge of a sanitation battalion in Louisiana.

JOHN WARD-Sergeant Ward, whose true name was John Warrior, was a Seminole Freedman of mixed Seminole and Negro blood serving as a scout for the 24th Infantry. On April 25, 1875, Ward and two other scouts commanded by a white Lieutenant attacked

25 Comanches on the Pecos River, Texas. When the officer was wounded, the scouts went back for him and saved his life. Ward and the other two scouts, Pompey Factor and Isaac Payne, were all awarded the Medal of Honor. At least 75 Seminole Freedmen were enlisted in the Army as Indian Scouts. They were renowned trackers and participated in at least 25 major engagements with hostile Indians but NONE were ever killed or wounded in these actions.

WILLIAM WILSON-Sgt. Wilson became the Army's second recipient of two Medals of Honor. While serving with Company I of the 4th U.S. Cavalry, his first Medal was awarded for pursuing a band of cattle thieves from New Mexico on March 28, 1872. His second Medal was awarded for leading his troop in a raid on a Comanche village when his commander became mired in quicksand on September 29 of the same year.

CHARLES WINDOLPH-As a 24-year-old Private with Company H of the 7th Cavalry, Windolph earned his Medal of Honor at the Battle of the Little Big Horn in Montana on June 25, 1876, the infamous "Custer's Last Stand" in which double Medal of Honor recipient Thomas Custer perished. Windolph died on March 11, 1950, at age 98 the last survivor of that battle.

LEONARD WOOD-As an Assistant Surgeon, Wood was awarded the Medal of Honor during actions against the Apache chief Geronimo in the summer of 1886. In 1898, Wood commanded the Army troops in Cuba during the Spanish-American War. He also served as Governor General of the Philippines, Army Chief of Staff and lost the 1920 Republican nomination for President of the United States to Warren G. Harding, who was elected. Fort Leonard Wood, Missouri, is named for him.

BRENT WOODS-A former slave, Woods served in Company B of the 9th Cavalry. In action against Apaches in New Mexico on August 19, 1881, Sergeant Woods took charge of his company after the commander was killed and the second in command deserted under fire. He was awarded the Medal of Honor in 1894, retired from the Army in 1902 and returned to his home in Pulaski County, Kentucky. He died there in 1906 and was buried in obscurity. In 1989, he was re-interred in Mill Springs National Cemetery, Kentucky, with full military honors.

*The Certificate of Merit was established for Army privates during the Mexican War in 1847. In 1854, non-commissioned officers were made eligible. Originally a certificate, it was awarded to a soldier for "having distinguished himself in the services of the United States in battle or peacetime, for heroism involving saving life or property at the risk of one's own or for other services that the President of the United States thought were deserving of this certificate."

In 1905, an actual medal was issued to former recipients. In 1918, this medal was discontinued and it could be exchanged for a Distinguished Service Medal. In 1934, this was changed and it could be exchanged for a Distinguished Service Cross, the second-highest award for combat valor.

Korean Campaign
1871

NAVY-9 awards to 9 individuals, all new recipients. None were posthumous.

MARINE CORPS-6 awards to 6 individuals, all new recipients. None were posthumous.

TOTAL-15 awards to 15 individuals, all new recipients. None were posthumous.

These Medals were awarded for actions on June 9-11, 1871, after Koreans destroyed the American freighter *General Sherman* and massacred her crew. After the Asiatic Squadron arrived in Korean waters, three Korean forts along the Han River fired upon American gunboats. On June 10, Rear Admiral John Rodgers landed a force of 651 men including 109 Marines to attack the forts. The forts were taken in two days of hand-to-hand fighting. The resulting 15 Medals of Honor were all issued within the next 18 months with the exception of one that was not awarded until December 4, 1915, 44 years later.

Another interesting aside is the fact that four of the nine Navy citations mention a "Lt. McKee", who evidently performed just as heroically as his men but naval officers were not eligible for the Medal of Honor at that time.

BY RANK:

NAVY

Chief Quartermaster	1	Quartermaster	2
Boatswains Mate	1	Carpenter	1
Landsman	2	Ordinary Seaman	2

MARINE CORPS

Corporal	1
Private	5

MOST DECORATED UNITS (NAVY)		MOST DECORATED UNITS (MARINES)	
U.S.S. *Colorado*	5	U.S.S. *Colorado*	3
U.S.S. *Benicia*	2	U.S.S. *Alaska*	1
		U.S.S. *Carondelet*	1
		U.S.S. *Benecia*	1

AGE OF RECIPIENTS:

50-59	1
40-49	0
30-39	6
20-29	7
Unknown	1

AVERAGE AGE:	30

YOUNGEST RECIPIENT:

Navy Ordinary Seaman William Troy was born on an undetermined date in 1848 and was either 22 or 23 years old when he earned his Medal on June 11, 1871.

OLDEST RECIPIENT:

Navy Ordinary Seaman John Andrews, born on an undetermined date in 1821, was either 49 or 50 years old when he earned his Medal on June 9-10, 1871.

NOTABLE INDIVIDUALS:

JOHN COLEMAN-This action provided the first known instance of a Medal of Honor awarded to a man for saving the life of another Medal of Honor recipient when Marine Private John Coleman was cited for saving the life of Navy Boatswains Mate Alexander McKenzie on June 11, 1871.

WILLIAM F. LUKES-Navy Landsman Lukes received his Medal of Honor for the fighting inside the Korean forts on June 9-10, 1871. His citation states he "received a severe cut over the head". In fact he received 18 sword and spear wounds, was unconscious for 39 days afterwards and was an invalid for the rest of his life.

Non-Combat Actions
1871-1898

NAVY-101 awards to 98 individuals, 97 new recipients and 1 double recipient who earned his first Medal during the Civil War. Three new recipients were double recipients. None were posthumous.

MARINE CORPS-2 awards to 2 individuals, both new recipients. Neither was posthumous.

TOTAL-103 awards to 100 individuals, 99 new recipients, 3 new double award recipients and 1 double recipient who earned his first Medal during the Civil War. None were posthumous.

BY RANK:

NAVY:

Seaman	24
Ordinary Seaman	13
Landsmen	13
Boatswains Mate	8
Captain of the Top	5
Fireman First Class	5
Fireman Second Class	3
Quartermaster	3
Coxswain	2
Apprentice	2
Boilermaker	1
Master at Arms	1
Captain of the Afterguard	1
Ordinary Seaman Apprentice	1
Captain of the Hold	1
Quartergunner	1
Captain of the Mizzentop	1
Seaman Apprentice 2/c	1
Carpenters Mate	1

Second Class Boy	1
Chief Boatswains Mate	1
Ships Cook	1
Chief Quartergunner	1
Ships Cook First Class	1
Cooper	1
Ships Corporal	1
Gunners Mate	1
Ships Printer	1
Gunners Mate Third Class	1
Watertender	1

MARINE CORPS:

Corporal	2

Of the 101 Navy awards, 83 were for rescuing shipmates from drowning. These awards involved 48 different ships, with multiple awards on 24 of them. The most were awarded to sailors on the U.S.S. *Plymouth* (8) and the U.S.S. *Kansas* (6). Four of the Navy awards (to three men including one double recipient) were to black sailors. The two Marine awards were also for rescuing drowning shipmates on two different ships.

BY LOCATION OF ACTION:

Unknown	19
Virginia	10
New York	8
Rhode Island	7
California	4
District of Columbia	3
Pennsylvania	2
Delaware River	1
Maryland	1
Massachusetts	1
Louisiana	1
South Carolina	1

Nicaragua	6
France	7
Brazil	4
Peru	4
China	3
Egypt	2
Mexico	2
Portugal	2
Germany	2
Liberia	2
Italy	2
Samoa	1
Chile	1
Hawaii	1
Greenland	1
Nova Scotia	1
Uruguay	1
Minorca	1

BLACK RECIPIENTS:

Six black sailors received seven Medals of Honor during this period. One became the only black double recipient.

AGE OF RECIPIENTS:

50-59	1
40-49	3
30-39	21
20-29	63
Age 19	1
Age 18	3
Age 17	4
Age 16	1
Unknown	3
AVERAGE AGE:	26

YOUNGEST RECIPIENT:

Navy Apprentice John Hayden, born in 1863, was either 15 or 16 years old when he earned his Medal for rescuing a shipmate from drowning on July 15, 1879.

OLDEST RECIPIENT:

Navy Seaman Antonio Williams, born in Malta in 1825, was either 51 or 52 years old when he earned his Medal on November 24, 1877.

NOTABLE INDIVIDUALS:

ROBERT SWEENEY-Ordinary Seaman Sweeney, born in the West Indies, is the only black man to earn two Medals of Honor, both for saving drowning shipmates. His first Medal was awarded for saving a man on October 26, 1881, aboard the U.S.S. *Kearsarge* and the second was awarded for another rescue on December 20, 1883, aboard the U.S.S. *Jamestown*. His three-year enlistment expired in September of 1884 and he left the service.

ALBERT WEISBOGEL-Captain of the Mizzentop Weisbogel was awarded two Medals of Honor for saving shipmates from drowning. The first was on January 11, 1874, while serving aboard the U.S.S. *Benicia* and the second was on April 27, 1876, on board the U.S.S. *Plymouth*. At 4 feet, 11 inches tall, he is the smallest of all double recipients and doubtlessly a contender for the smallest of all recipients.

LOUIS WILLIAMS-Captain of the Hold Williams was the third Navy man during this period awarded two Medals of Honor for saving drowning shipmates. The first was on March 16, 1883, aboard the U.S.S. *Lackawanna* in Honolulu, Hawaii, and the second was on June 13, 1884, aboard the same ship in Callao, Peru. He died on February 20, 1886.

Spanish-American War
1898

ARMY-31 awards to 31 individuals, all new recipients, 1 posthumous.

NAVY-64 awards to 64 individuals, all new recipients, none posthumous.

MARINE CORPS-15 awards to 15 individuals, all new recipients, none posthumous.

TOTAL-110 awards to 110 individuals, all new recipients, 1 posthumous.

This "splendid little war" (in the words of Secretary of State John Hay) began when the battleship U.S.S *Maine* exploded in Havana harbor on February 15, 1898. An investigation concluded that the cause was a mine. Historians have since disputed that conclusion and it may have been an accidental boiler explosion. At any rate, on April 20, President McKinley demanded that Spain withdraw from Cuba. On April 22, the U.S. Navy blockaded Cuban ports and three days later war was declared.

A U.S. Navy fleet under Admiral George Dewey destroyed the Spanish fleet in the Philippines on May 1 and captured Guam on June 20.

An Army force of about 17,000 men was landed near Santiago, Cuba, on June 22-27, 1898. Among them were the 1st Volunteer Cavalry (known as the Rough Riders) under previous Medal recipient Colonel Leonard Wood and Lt. Col. Theodore Roosevelt. The Army attacked Santiago on July 1 and the Navy began a bombardment on July 3. The city surrendered on July 17.

Puerto Rico was invaded on July 25 and an armistice was signed on August 12.

The American forces suffered a total of 487 killed—29 officers and 440 enlisted men in the Army, 1 officer and 17 enlisted men in the Navy.

On December 10, 1898, Spain ceded the Philippines, Guam

and Puerto Rico to the U.S. and approved independence for Cuba.

BY RANK:

ARMY

Lt. Colonel	1	(1)
Captain	1	
1st Lt.	2	
2nd Lt.	2	
Asst. Surgeon	1	
Sgt. Major	1	
Sergeant	2	
Corporal	3	
Private	17	
Musician	1	

MARINES

Sergeant	2
Private	13

NAVY

Lieutenant	1
Apprentice 1/c	3
Blacksmith	2
Boatswains Mate 1/c	1
Boatswains Mate 2/c	2
Carpenters Mate 3/c	1
Chief Boatswains Mate	1
Chief Carpenters Mate	2
Chief Gunners Mate	1
Chief Machinist	2
Chief Master at Arms	1
Coal Passer	1
Coppersmith	1

Coxswain	8
Fireman 1/c	5
Fireman 2/c	1
Gunners Mate 1/c	3
Gunners Mate 2/c	1
Gunners Mate 3/c	1
Landsman	2
Machinist 1/c	2
Mate	1
Oiler	1
Ordinary Seaman	4
Sailmakers Mate	1
Seaman	13
Watertender	2

BY LOCATION OF ACTION:

Cuba	104
Philippine Islands	4
Unknown	2

MOST DECORATED UNITS:

ARMY/REGIMENTAL LEVEL

17th Infantry	9
10th Cavalry	5
10th Infantry	5

ARMY/COMPANY LEVEL

Co. H., 21st Infantry	6

NAVY/MARINE CORPS

U.S.S. *Nashville*	28 (21 Navy and 7 Marines)
U.S.S. *Marblehead*	24 (19 Navy and 5 Marines)

BLACK RECIPIENTS:

Seven black men received the Medal of Honor during the Spanish-American War. Six were enlisted men with the all-black 10th Cavalry and one was an enlisted man in the Navy.

AGE OF RECIPIENTS:

40-49	6
30-39	42
20-29	55
Age 19	4
Age 18	2
Unknown	1

AVERAGE AGE: 28

YOUNGEST RECIPIENT:

Navy Apprentice William Levery was born on June 30, 1879, and was the younger of two 18-year-old Medal recipients when he earned his Medal while serving on the U.S.S. *Marblehead* at Cienfuegos, Cuba, on May 11, 1898. Strangely enough, this was on the same date and same ship as the_

OLDEST RECIPIENT:

Navy Chief Boatswains Mate James Harvey Bennett, born April 5, 1851, was 47 when he earned his Medal on the U.S.S. *Marblehead* on May 11, 1898.

NOTABLE INDIVIDUALS:

JAMES ROBB CHURCH-Assistant Surgeon Church (later Colonel) earned his Medal by rescuing several wounded men under fire at Las Guasimas, Cuba, on June 24, 1898. A member of the 1st U.S. Volunteer Cavalry, Church was presented his Medal on January 10, 1906, by his former commanding officer, then-President Theodore Roosevelt.

This was only the third award of the Medal of Honor known to be personally presented by a President of the United States. President Lincoln had presented one in 1864 and Roosevelt had presented one in 1904. This was the first award made after Roosevelt had issued an Executive Order stating that "the Medal should be presented at the White House by the President as Commander-in-Chief whenever possible." During wartime, the award was to be presented by a Division Commander or higher. This significantly raised the prestige associated with a Medal of Honor award.

Ninety-five years and six days later, Roosevelt himself was honored posthumously with the award. It is highly unlikely that this set of circumstances will ever be repeated.

JOHN J. DORAN-Navy Boatswains Mate Second Class Doran was one of 24 men aboard the U.S.S. *Marblehead* to receive Medals of Honor during this conflict. His nephew, Charles Watters, would be awarded the Medal of Honor for his service in Vietnam 69 years later.

RICHARD PEARSON HOBSON-Hobson entered the U.S. Naval Academy in 1885 at the age of 15. On June 3, 1898, while serving as a Lieutenant on the U.S.S. *Merrimac* at Santiago de Cuba, Hobson performed the first action for which a naval officer received the Medal of Honor.

Navy and Marine Corps officers were not eligible for the Medal of Honor until legislation in March of 1915. Hobson retired from the Navy in 1903 and served four terms as a Democratic Congressman from Alabama. He was awarded his Medal in 1933.

JOHN HENRY QUICK-Marine Sergeant Quick received his Medal of Honor for actions during the battle of Cuzco, Cuba, on June 14, 1898. He was recommended for a second Medal of Honor in the Philippines in 1901 but it was rejected. As though to prove it was no accident, he was awarded the Navy Cross and Army Distinguished Service Cross during his service in World War I.

THEODORE ROOSEVELT-In one of the most recent awards, on January 16, 2001, Lieutenant Colonel Roosevelt was posthumously awarded the Medal of Honor for his actions on San Juan Hill. See Most Recent Awards.

GEORGE H. WANTON-Private Wanton of Troop M, 10th Cavalry, is listed in some publications as the first black man to receive the Medal of Honor. As we have already seen, this is not true (see Robert Blake and William Carney in the Civil War section). He was one of 7 black medal recipients for the Spanish-American War.

SAMOAN CAMPAIGN
1899

NAVY-1 award to 1 individual, a new recipient, not posthumous.

MARINE CORPS-3 awards to 3 individuals, all new recipients, none posthumous.

TOTAL-4 awards to 4 individuals, all new recipients, none posthumous.

Beginning in 1847, Great Britain, Germany and the United States all claimed the Samoa Islands. The machinations of the three major powers led to decades of civil war between the islanders with each of the powers backing their own chieftain. Eventually Britain and the U.S. became allied against Germany and the situation became more bellicose. On March 15, 1899, American and British ships attacked the German-supported chieftain by bombarding the Samoan city of Apia. An Anglo-American invasion force followed this.

On April 1, 1899, a force of 62 British and 56 Americans were ambushed by 800 Samoan warriors and resulted in the battle of Tagalii. The situation eventually stabilized with the major powers controlling the cities and the rebels controlling the rural areas. In November, a treaty was drawn up that divided the islands among the three powers.

Four Medals of Honor were awarded as a result of the battle of Tagalii.

BY RANK:

NAVY

Gunners Mate First Class	1

MARINES

Sergeant	2
Private	1

AGE OF RECIPIENTS:

30-39	2
20-29	2

AVERAGE AGE: 31

YOUNGEST RECIPIENT:

Navy Gunners Mate First Class was born June 3, 1872, and was 26 years old at the time of his Medal of Honor action.

OLDEST RECIPIENT:

Marine Sergeant Michael Joseph McNally, born June 29, 1830, was 39 at the time of his Medal of Honor action.

NOTABLE INDIVIDUALS:

HENRY LEWIS HULBERT-Marine Private Hulbert, 32, was a member of the Marine Guard from the ship U.S.S. *Philadelphia* and was cited for his actions while fighting a rear guard action during the battle of Tagalii. A career Marine, 19 years later Hulbert was a First Lieutenant and earned a Navy Cross at Belleau Wood during World War I. He was killed in action at Mont Blanc, France, in October of 1918.

PHILIPPINE INSURRECTION
1899-1902

ARMY-69 awards to 69 individuals, all new recipients, 4 posthumous.

NAVY-5 awards to 5 individuals, all new recipients, none posthumous.

MARINE CORPS-6 awards to 6 individuals, all new recipients, none posthumous.

TOTAL-80 awards to 80 individuals, all new recipients, 4 posthumous.

On February 4, 1899, Filipino insurgents attempting to win independence from the U.S. started a guerilla war. The leader of the insurgency, Emilio Aguinaldo, was captured on May 23, 1901, but sporadic fighting continued into 1902.

BY RANK:

ARMY		NAVY		MARINES	
Colonel	2	Coxswain	1	Captain	2
Lt. Col.	3	Gunners Mate 2/c	1	Sergeant	1
Major	3 (1)	Gunners Mate 3/c	1	Corporal	1
Captain	8 (1)	Seaman	1	Private	2
1st Lt.	9	Ordinary Seaman	1		
2nd Lt.	6				
Sergeant	7				
Corporal	5				
Private	24 (2)				
Artificer	2				

MOST DECORATED UNITS:

ARMY

36th Infantry Division	11

1st North Dakota Volunteer Infantry	9
6th Cavalry	4

AGE OF RECIPIENTS:

50-59	1
40-49	8
30-39	20
20-29	46
Age 19	3
Age 18	1
Unknown	1

AVERAGE AGE:	29

YOUNGEST RECIPIENT:

Navy Seaman Andrew Peter Forbeck, born August 29, 1881, was 18 when he earned his Medal on July 16, 1900.

OLDEST RECIPIENT:

Army Captain William Edward Birkhimer, born March 1, 1848, was 51 years old when he earned his Medal on May 13, 1899.

NOTABLE INDIVIDUALS:

HIRAM IDDINGS BEARSS-Marine Colonel (then a Captain) Bearss received his Medal of Honor for multiple actions in the Philippines in 1901 and 1902. Known as "Hiking Hiram" because of his long-range recons behind enemy lines, he also served in the Boxer Rebellion in China, at Vera Cruz, in the Dominican Republic and in World War I in which he won a Distinguished Service Cross while receiving a spinal injury. He retired as a Colonel in 1918 after 21 years of service and 11 decorations for valor.

WEBB C. HAYES-Lt. Colonel Hayes of the 31st Infantry received his Medal of Honor for action on Luzon in 1899. His father, Rutherford B. Hayes, was President of the United States in 1877-1881.

DAVID DIXON PORTER-Marine Captain Porter earned his Medal of Honor in the same action as Captain Hiram Bearss (above). Porter was a scion of one of the most prestigious families in American military history with six generations of military service to its credit. His great-grandfather was Navy Commodore David Porter (1780-1843) who fought in the Barbary Wars and the War of 1812. Capt. Porter was the namesake of his even more illustrious grandfather. Navy Admiral David Dixon Porter (1813-1891) served in the Civil War, was Superintendent of the U.S. Naval Academy and retired as a full admiral. Capt. Porter's father retired from the Marine Corps as a Lieutenant Colonel. Capt. Porter's Medal was not presented until 1934. He retired from the Marines as a Major General and died in 1944 at the age of 66.

China Relief Expedition-Boxer Rebellion
1900

ARMY-4 awards to 4 individuals, all new recipients, none posthumous.

NAVY-22 awards to 22 individuals, all new recipients, none posthumous.

MARINE CORPS-33 awards to 33 individuals, all new recipients, 1 posthumous.

TOTAL-59 awards to 59 individuals, all new recipients, 1 posthumous.

In 1900, societies in China known as "Boxers" were organized in opposition to foreign aggression. The resulting patriotic fervor led to a series of attacks against all foreigners and a siege of the British Embassy where many alien residents had taken refuge.

A naval force of sailors, marines and soldiers landed in May to protect the foreign citizens and embassies. A major battle was fought at Tientsin and Peking endured a 55-day siege. The rebellion ended on August 13, 1900.

BY RANK:

ARMY

Captain	1
1st Lt.	1
Private	1
Musician	1

MARINES

Gunnery Sergeant	1
Sergeant	4
Corporal	4

Private	23 (1)
Drummer	1

NAVY

Boatswains Mate 1/c	2
Chief Boatswains Mate	1
Chief Carpenters Mate	1
Chief Machinist	1
Coxswain	4
Gunners Mate 1/c	1
Gunners Mate 2/c	1
Gunners Mate 3/c	1
Hospital Apprentice	1
Landsman	2
Machinist 1/c	1
Oiler	1
Ordinary Seaman	2
Seaman	3

MOST DECORATED UNITS:

ARMY

9th U.S. Infantry	3

AGE OF RECIPIENTS:

40-49	2
30 39	12
20 29	42
Age 19	3

AVERAGE AGE: 27

YOUNGEST RECIPIENT:

Navy Hospital Apprentice Robert Henry Stanley, born May 2, 1881, was 19 when he earned his Medal on June 13-22, 1900.

OLDEST RECIPIENT:

Marine Gunnery Sergeant Peter Stewart, born February 17, 1858, was 42 years old when he earned his Medal on June 13-22, 1900.

NOTABLE INDIVIDUALS:

CALVIN PEARL TITUS-On August 14, 1900, Musician Titus was the first soldier to scale the 30-foot wall of the city of Peking, proving the feasibility of such an assault by not using ropes or ladders. He was appointed to West Point by President McKinley and awarded his Medal of Honor in 1902 by President Theodore Roosevelt, making him the only West Point freshman to wear a Medal of Honor. Titus graduated in 1905 and later retired from the Army as a Lieutenant Colonel.

Non-Combat Actions
1899-1910

NAVY-49 awards to 48 individuals, all new recipients, one double award, none posthumous.

MARINE CORPS-2 awards to 2 individuals, both new recipients, neither posthumous.

TOTAL-51 awards to 50 individuals, all new recipients, none posthumous.

At the turn of the century, the U.S. Navy experienced a number of serious mishaps aboard their vessels and this is reflected in their non-combat awards for that period. Of the 50 awards chronicled during this period, only 9 were for saving drowning shipmates. The remainder were for responding to shipwrecks, fires and explosions. Awards were given on 18 different ships with multiple awards on 8 of them. The only two given on land were for responding to a fire in Coquimbo, Chile. The most rewarded mishap was the explosion of a boiler on the U.S.S. *Bennington* in San Diego harbor on July 21, 1905. A boiler explosion followed on the U.S.S. *Iowa* on January 25 of the same year and a fire aboard the U.S.S. *North Dakota* on September 8, 1910.

BY RANK:

NAVY

Boatswains Mate	2	Quartermaster 3/c	2
Boatswains Mate 1/c	2	Seaman	7
Boilermaker	1	Seaman 1/c	1
Carpenters Mate 2/c	1	Shipfitter 1/c	1
Chief Boatswain	1	Ships Cook 1/c	1
Chief Carpenters Mate	1	Watertender	5
Chief Electrician	1	Chief Gunner	1
Chief Gunners Mate	2	Chief Bosns Mate	1
Chief Machinist	1	Chief Master/Arms	1
Chief Machinists Mate	2	Chief Watertender	4

Coxswain	2	Fireman 1/c	3
Gunners Mate 1/c	1	Hospital Steward	1
Machinists Mate 1/c	2	Ordinary Seaman	1

MARINES

Sergeant	1
Private	1

MOST DECORATED UNITS:

U.S.S. *Bennington*	11
U.S.S. *Iowa*	6
U.S.S. *North Dakota*	6
U.S.S. *Missouri*	5
U.S.S. *Leyden*	4
U.S.S. *Petrel*	3
U.S.S. *Hopkins*	2
U.S.S. *Kearsarge*	2

1 award each on 10 other vessels.

AGE OF RECIPIENTS:

50-59	2
40-49	2
30-39	16
20-29	27
Age 19	1
Unknown	2

AVERAGE AGE: 29

YOUNGEST RECIPIENT:

Navy Quartermaster Third Class Raymond Erwin Davis, born September 19, 1885, was 19 when he earned his Medal on the U.S.S. *Bennington* on July 21, 1905.

OLDEST RECIPIENT:

Navy Chief Carpenter's Mate Robert Klein, born November 11, 1848, was 55 when he earned his Medal on the U.S.S. *Raleigh* on January 25, 1904.

NOTABLE INDIVIDUALS:

JOHN KING-Navy Watertender King was the only double award recipient during this period, both for heroism during boiler mishaps but on different ships. His first award was for actions on the U.S.S. *Vicksburg* on May 29, 1901, and the second was on the U.S.S. *Salem* on September 13, 1909. He died in 1938 at the age of 76.

Actions Against Outlaws-Philippine Islands
1911

ARMY-1 award to 1 individual, a new recipient, not posthumous.

NAVY-5 awards to 5 individuals, all new recipients, none posthumous.

TOTAL-6 awards to 6 individuals, all new recipients, none posthumous.

All the Navy awards were to men from the U.S.S. *Pampang* who were on a shore party on September 24, 1911, that became involved in a firefight with 20 Moro natives.

The Army award was to a Private in the same action on the same date.

BY RANK:

NAVY		ARMY	
Carpenters Mate 3/c	1	Private	1
Hospital Apprentice	1		
Machinists Mate 2/c	1		
Ordinary Seaman	1		
Seaman	1		

AVERAGE AGE:	22

YOUNGEST RECIPIENT:

Navy Hospital Apprentice Fred Henry McGuire, born November 7, 1890, was 20 when he earned his Medal on September 24, 1911.

OLDEST RECIPIENT:

Navy Machinist's Mate Second Class George Francis Henrechon, born November 22, 1885, was 25 when he earned his Medal on September 24, 1911.

NOTABLE INDIVIDUALS:

JOSE B. NISPEROS-Army Private Jose B. Nisperos was severely wounded during the battle. His left arm was broken and he received several spear wounds. Unable to stand, he continued firing his rifle with one hand keeping the party from being overrun.

Nisperos was the first Filipino to be awarded the Medal of Honor, the first Asia-Pacific recipient and the last one until World War II.

MEXICAN CAMPAIGN
(VERA CRUZ)
1914

ARMY-1 award to 1 individual, a new recipient, not posthumous.

NAVY-46 awards to 45 individuals, 44 new recipients and one a former recipient from the 1900 China Relief Expedition, none posthumous.

MARINE CORPS-9 awards to 9 individuals, all new recipients, none posthumous.

TOTAL-56 awards to 55 individuals, 54 new recipients and one former recipient from the 1900 China Expedition, none posthumous.

On April 6, 1914, a group of U.S. Navy sailors were arrested off of an American boat in Tampico, Mexico, and marched through the streets. An American admiral demanded an apology, which was not forthcoming. On April 22, Congress authorized President Wilson to use American forces. A regiment of Marines and a battalion of sailors were landed at Vera Cruz and cleared the city in two days of fighting, April 21 and 22. Casualties were 15 Americans killed and 56 wounded. Fifty-six Medals of Honor were awarded for this action.

BY RANK:

ARMY

Captain	1

MARINES

Lt. Colonel	1
Major	4
Captain	4

NAVY

Rear Admiral	1	Commander	3
Captain	3	Lieutenant	11
Lt. Commander	2	Ensign	6
Lieutenant j.g.	2	Boatswains Mate 2/c	3
Surgeon	2	Chief Gunner	1
Chief Boatswain	1	Coxswain	1
Chief Gunners Mate	1	Hospital Apprentice 1/c	1
Electrician 3/c	1	Quartermaster 2/c	1
Ordinary Seaman	2		
Seaman	4		

These were the first Medals of Honor awarded after Navy and Marine Corps officers became eligible on March 3, 1915.

MOST DECORATED UNITS:

U.S.S. *Florida*	13
U.S.S. *Utah*	3

AGE OF RECIPIENTS:

The average age rose in this conflict because this was the first conflict in which Navy and Marine Corps officers were eligible for the Medal of Honor. As a result, a number of older, senior commanders received awards.

50-59	4
40-49	8
30-39	20
20-29	21
Age 19	1
Age 18	1
Age 16	1
AVERAGE AGE:	32

YOUNGEST RECIPIENT:

Navy Seaman James Aloysius Walsh, born July 24, 1897, was 16 when he earned his Medal on April 21-22, 1914.

OLDEST RECIPIENT:

Navy Rear Admiral Frank Friday Fletcher, born November 23, 1855, was 58 when he earned his Medal as commander of the naval task force at Vera Cruz on April 21-22, 1914.

NOTABLE INDIVIDUALS:

SMEDLEY DARLINGTON BUTLER-The son of a Quaker U.S. Congressman, Butler was commissioned as a 2nd Lieutenant in the Spanish-American War at the age of 16. He became the only Marine officer to receive two Medals of Honor, the first as a Major at Vera Cruz in 1914 and the second in Haiti the following year. Previously Butler had also seen combat in the Philippines and China. For actions in China, he received the Brevet Medal, which would have probably been a third Medal of Honor except Marine officers were not eligible for the Medal at that time. When he received his first Medal of Honor for Vera Cruz, he returned it to the Navy Department because he felt it was undeserved. He was ordered to keep it.

In 1918, Butler became a Brigadier General at the age of 38 and, in 1929, at the age of 48, a Major General, both the youngest in Marine history. His public criticism of Benito Mussolini caused him to become the first general officer to be arrested since the Civil War. The charges were dropped but Butler was passed over for Commandant of the Marine Corps in 1930. He retired the next year after serving 33 years, participating in 14 battles and receiving 17 medals. He died at age 58 in 1940 in Philadelphia.

ALBERTUS WRIGHT CATLIN-Marine Major Catlin received his Medal of Honor as a battalion commander at Vera Cruz. An Annapolis graduate, as a First Lieutenant Catlin had been in command of the Marine detail on the USS *Maine* when it was sunk in

Havana harbor in 1898, the action which started the Spanish-American War. Later wounded at Belleau Wood in World War I, he retired as a Brigadier General.

FRANK JACK FLETCHER-While commanding the U.S.S. *Esperanze* at Vera Cruz as a 28-year-old Lieutenant, Fletcher was awarded his Medal of Honor. A Medal of Honor was also awarded to his uncle, Rear Admiral Frank Friday Fletcher, who was the commander of the naval task force at Vera Cruz. Later rising to the rank of Admiral himself, Frank Jack Fletcher commanded the aircraft carrier U.S.S. *Yorktown* in the Battle of the Coral Sea and at Midway in 1942. Both the carriers *Yorktown* and *Lexington* were sunk while under his command in World War II. He died on April 25, 1973, four days before his 88th birthday.

JOHN McCLOY-Navy Chief Boatswain McCloy was awarded his second Medal for this action. His first had been as a Coxswain assigned to the U.S.S. *Newark* during the China Relief Expedition in June of 1900. He died on May 25, 1945, at the age of 69.

WENDELL CUSHING NEVILLE-Lt. Colonel Neville, an Annapolis classmate of Albertus Catlin, received his Medal of Honor while serving as the commander of the 2nd Marine Regiment at Vera Cruz. He later served as a Colonel and Brigadier General in World War I. As a Major General, he was Commandant of the Marine Corps in 1929-1930 before his death on July 8, 1930.

HAITIAN CAMPAIGN
1915

MARINE CORPS-6 awards to 6 individuals, 4 new recipients and 2 to previous recipients; one for the 1900 China Relief Expedition and one for the Vera Cruz Campaign. None posthumous.

TOTAL-6 awards to 6 individuals, 4 new recipients and 2 to previous recipients. None posthumous.

In October and November of 1915, native Caco guerrillas were terrorizing the peaceful natives in Haiti. A naval task force was sent to the island and Marines were landed to pacify the situation. Major battles erupted at Fort Liberte on October 24 and Fort Riviere on November 17. Three Medals of Honor were awarded for each battle, two of them being second awards to previous recipients.

BY RANK:

MARINES

Major	1
Captain	1
1st Lieutenant	1
Gunnery Sergeant	1
Sergeant	1
Private	1

AGE OF RECIPIENTS:

40-49	1
30-39	4
20-29	1

AVERAGE AGE: 33

YOUNGEST RECIPIENT:

Marine Private Samuel Gross (true name: Samuel Marguilies) born May 9, 1891, was 24 when he earned his Medal on November 17, 1915.

OLDEST RECIPIENT:

Marine Gunnery Sergeant Daniel Joseph Daly, born November 11, 1873, was 41 when he earned his second Medal of Honor on October 24, 1915. (see below)

NOTABLE INDIVIDUALS:

DANIEL JOSEPH DALY-Dan Daly became a justifiable Marine Corps legend. At 5'6" and 130 pounds, he was a little bigger than a future Army legend named Audie Murphy but still proved that dynamite came in small packages. He was the only Marine enlisted man to earn two Medals of Honor for separate actions and, among all double Medal recipients, only one other (Navy Fireman John Lafferty/Laverty) earned his Medals farther apart.

Born on November 11, 1873, in Glen Cove, Long Island, he enlisted at age 25. He was awarded his first Medal of Honor barely 19 months after his enlistment. It was for heroism displayed over 8 weeks during the summer of 1900 during the Boxer Rebellion in Peking, China. Daly allegedly killed over 200 Chinese during these actions.

Daly's second Medal came on October 22, 1915, for actions in Haiti. In World War I, he was recommended for a third Medal of Honor in June of 1918 but it was denied, evidently only because higher military authority felt no one should have three of them. He was awarded the Navy Cross, the Army's Distinguished Service Cross and the French *Medaille Militaire*. He also firmly entrenched himself in Marine legend when he led a charge by yelling back at his men "Come on you sons-of-bitches, do you want to live forever?"

Daly retired from the Marines in 1919 after a very active 20 years of service, spent the next 17 years as a bank guard and died from a heart attack in New York in 1937 at the age of 63.

Non-Combat Actions
1915-1916

NAVY-8 awards to 8 individuals, all new recipients, one posthumous.

TOTAL-8 awards to 8 individuals, all new recipients, one posthumous.

These awards were made to sailors on four different ships. Multiple awards were made on two ships—three awards on the U.S.S. *Memphis* during a hurricane in Santo Domingo on August 29, 1916, and two for an explosion on the U.S.S. *San Diego* on January 21, 1915. Single awards were made on the U.S.S. *Decatur*, U.S.S. *New York* and to a diver rescuing another diver during the sinking of the U.S.S. *F-4*.

BY RANK:

NAVY

Lt. Commander	1
Lieutenant	1
Chief Gunners Mate	1
Chief Machinists Mate	1 (1)
Chief Watertender	1
Fireman 2/c	1
Gunners Mate 1/c	1
Machinist	1

BY LOCATION OF ACTION:

Unknown	4
Caribbean Sea	3
Pacific Ocean	1

AGE OF RECIPIENTS:

40-49	2
30-39	3
20-29	3

AVERAGE AGE: 32

YOUNGEST RECIPIENT:

Navy Lieutenant Commander Robert Webster Cary, born August 18, 1890, was 24 when he earned his Medal as an Ensign on the U.S.S. *San Diego* on January 21, 1915.

OLDEST RECIPIENT:

Navy Gunner's Mate First Class Wilhelm Smith, born April 10, 1870, was 45 when he earned his Medal on the U.S.S. *New York* on January 24, 1916.

NOTABLE INDIVIDUALS:

GEORGE WILLIAM RUD-Chief Machinists Mate Rud was 33 when he served on the U.S.S. *Memphis* during its destruction in a hurricane off Santo Domingo on August 29, 1916. As sea water poured into the engine room, Rud remained at his post until scalded to death by steam, thus proving that peacetime service can be just as deadly as combat.

DOMINICAN CAMPAIGN
1916

MARINE CORPS-3 awards to 3 individuals, all new recipients, none posthumous.

TOTAL-3 awards to 3 individuals, all new recipients, none posthumous.

The American ambassador requested help during a revolution in the Dominican Republic on May 3, 1916. Two days later, two companies of Marines and a detachment of sailors were landed. Three Medals of Honor were awarded for operations over the next six months.

BY RANK:

MARINES

1st Lieutenant	1
First Sergeant	1
Corporal	1

AGE OF RECIPIENTS:

20-29	3

AVERAGE AGE: 27

YOUNGEST RECIPIENT:

Marine Corporal Joseph Anthony Glowin, born March 14, 1892, was 24 when he earned his Medal on July 3, 1916.

OLDEST RECIPIENT:

Marine First Lieutenant Ernest Calvin Williams, born August

2, 1887, was 29 when he earned his Medal on November 29, 1916. (see below)

NOTABLE INDIVIDUALS:

ERNEST CALVIN WILLIAMS-Marine First Lieutenant Williams received his Medal of Honor for attacking a rebel fortress with only a dozen Marines, continuing the attack after eight of them were wounded. He later won the Navy Cross, Army Distinguished Service Cross and French *Croix de Guerre* in World War I.

Crippled when a horse fell with him in 1921, Williams received a disability retirement. When Charles Lindbergh received the Medal of Honor in 1927 while a civilian and for non-combat actions, Williams was very vocally critical. In protest, he never wore his Medal of Honor again. He died from a cerebral hemorrhage in New York on April 11, 1940.

ROSWELL WINANS-As a First Sergeant, Winans was awarded the Medal of Honor for his actions in the Dominican Republic on July 3, 1916. Commissioned as an officer, he later served as a Captain in World War I, winning two Silver Stars and the French *Croix de Guerre*. He served as a Lieutenant Colonel in China in 1937 and retired as a Brigadier General.

WORLD WAR I
1917-1918

ARMY-90 awards to 90 individuals, all new recipients, 27 post-humous.

NAVY-21 awards to 21 individuals, all new recipients, 2 posthumous.

MARINE CORPS-13 awards to 8 individuals, 8 new recipients, 4 posthumous. Five (5) Marines received both the Army and Navy Medals of Honor for a single act of heroism.

TOTAL-124 awards to 119 individuals, 119 new recipients, 5 double awards, a total of 95 Army Medals and 29 Navy Medals awarded, 33 posthumous.

War had been raging in Europe since June of 1914 but America had remained isolated in spite of the loss of 128 American lives when a German submarine torpedoed the British liner Luisitania in 1915. Suffering from the British blockade, Germany declared unrestricted submarine warfare on January 31, 1917. The U.S. ended diplomatic relations with Germany on February 3 and declared war on April 6.

Marine regiments were assigned to Army Divisions. This unique mixture of service commands resulted in cross-awards of some decorations—some Marines were awarded both the Army Distinguished Service Cross and the Navy Cross, and five Marines were awarded both the Army and Navy Medals of Honor for single actions.

BY RANK:

ARMY		NAVY		MARINES	
Lt. Col.	3 (2)	Commander	1	2nd Lt.	1 (1)
Major	3 (1)	Lt. Commander	2	Gunnery Sgt.	3 (1)
Captain	7 (2)	Lieutenant	3	Sergeant	2 (1)

1st Lt	10 (2)	Lieutenant j.g.	1 (1)	Corporal	1 (1)
2nd Lt	6 (4)	Ensign	2	Private	1
1st Sgt	5 (1)	Boatswains Mate 2/c	1		
Sergeant	22 (4)	Chief Boatswains Mte	1		
Corporal	13 (4)	Chief Gunners Mte	1		
PFC	9 (3)	Chf.Machinists Mte	1		
Private	12 (4)	Gunners Mate 1/c	1 (1)		
		Hospital Apprntc 1/c	1		
		Pharmacists Mate 1/c	1		
		Quartermaster	1		
		Seaman	2		
		Ships Cook 3/c	1		
		Shipfitter 1/c	1		
TOTAL 90 (27)		21 (2)		8 (4)	

BY LOCATION OF ACTION:

France	102
Unknown	13
Belgium	2
Germany	1
Florida	1*

*This award is included in this section because it occurred during this conflict, it was a non-combat award related to wartime training and it doesn't fit in the interim periods before or after.

MOST DECORATED UNITS:

ARMY (DIVISION LEVEL)

30th Infantry Division	12
33rd Infantry Division	9
89th Infantry Division	9
77th Infantry Division	8

REGIMENTAL LEVEL

118th Inf., 30th Div	6
132nd Inf., 33rd Div	5
308th Inf., 77th Div	5
356th Inf., 89th Div	4

COMPANY LEVEL

Co. G, 118th Inf., 30th Div	2
Co. L, 354th Inf., 89th Div	2
Machine Gun Co., 107th Inf., 27th Div	2

ARMY AIR SERVICE-4 awards. Three were posthumous. Eddie Rickenbacker was the only World War I airman to live to receive his Medal of Honor.

NAVY-Awards were made to men on 8 separate ships, two each on the U.S.S. *Florence* and U.S.S. *Pittsburgh*. Three awards were for air missions. Six awards were to corpsmen and doctors serving on land with Marine units.

MARINES-During this war, some Marine units were administratively attached to larger Army headquarters, therefore making them subordinate to Army command and eligible for Army awards. As a result, some Marines received the Army Distinguished Service Cross and other decorations previously issued only to Army personnel.

Eight Marines received 13 Medals of Honor. Two Marine aviators received the Navy Medal, one Marine received only the Army Medal and five Marines received double awards of both the Army and Navy Medals for the same action. Two of the double award winners were posthumous. The sole marine officer to receive an award (posthumously) was one of the aviators.

AGE OF RECIPIENTS:

40-49	8
30-39	30

20-29	70
Age 19	5
Age 18	1
Unknown	5
AVERAGE AGE:	27

YOUNGEST RECIPIENT:

Army Private Calvin John Ward, born October 30, 1899, was 18 when he earned his Medal on October 8, 1918.

OLDEST RECIPIENT:

Army Major Joseph Henry Thompson, born September 26, 1871, was 47 when he earned his Medal on October 1, 1918.

NOTABLE INDIVIDUALS:

LOUIS CUKELA-A native of Serbia, Cukela served two years in the U.S. Army starting in 1914 and enlisted in the Marines after his discharge. As a tough-as-nails Gunnery Sergeant, he gained early fame for maiming the English language. One of his more famous sayings while chewing out subordinates who failed to accomplish their assignments was "Next time I send a goddamn fool, I go myself".

Cukela was one of five Marines who were awarded both the Army and Navy Medals of Honor for single actions during World War I, all for knocking out German machine gun nests. At Soissons in July of 1918, Cukela destroyed two machine gun nests using grenades and bayonet. His charge created another Marine legend— the surrendering Germans called him "*Teufelhund*"—Devil Dog— spreading the German name for American Marines as madmen who "killed everything that moved."

Cukela retired as a Major in 1940 but was recalled a month later for World War II, serving until 1946. He died in 1956 in Maryland.

WILLIAM JOSEPH DONOVAN-As a Lieutenant Colonel in the 165th Infantry, 42nd Infantry Division, Donovan was awarded the Medal of Honor for leading a charge against German machine guns during which he was wounded. He became the first American to hold the nation's three highest decorations (at that time); the Medal of Honor, Distinguished Service Cross and Distinguished Service Medal. He retired from the Army as a Major General and later became a founder of the American Legion but returned to create and command the Office of Special Services (OSS-the forerunner of the CIA) in World War II. In the 1950's, he received the first National Security Medal ever awarded. He died on February 8, 1959.

ERNEST AUGUST JANSON-Marine Gunnery Sergeant Janson was one of the Marines honored with both the Army and Navy Medals of Honor for a single action. He received the Navy Medal under his true name but he received the Army Medal under the false name of Charles F. Hoffman.

NELSON M. HOLDERMAN-Captain Holderman of the 307th Infantry, 77th Infantry Division, received his Medal of Honor for actions during a week when German soldiers surrounded his company. During that week, he was wounded 10 times.

MATEJ KOCAK-A Hungarian by birth, Marine Sergeant Kocak earned his Army and Navy Medals of Honor at Soissons on the same day, in the same battle and the same unit as Louis Cukela. He was killed in action three months later at Blanc Mont Ridge, the same battle in which the last two double recipients of the Medal of Honor (Marines Corporal John Henry Pruitt and Private John Joseph Kelly) earned their Medals.

FRANK LUKE JR.-Second Lieutenant Luke served only two months in combat with the Army Air Service in World War I but he made it count. He shot down 18 German planes in 18 days and the top American ace of the war, Eddie Rickenbacker, later called him "the greatest fighting pilot of the war." On September 29, 1918, Luke shot down 3 German balloons and strafed German ground troops. After being wounded and forced to land, he drew an automatic pistol and fought to the death against ground forces. Luke Air Force Base in Phoenix, Arizona, is named for him.

SAMUEL I. PARKER-Second Lieutenant Parker received his Medal of Honor for actions at Soissons, France, on July 18-19, 1918. He became the most decorated soldier of World War I. In addition to the Medal of Honor, he received the Distinguished Service Cross, two Silver Stars, two Purple Hearts, the Legion of Merit and the *Croix de Guerre.*

FRED W. STOCKHAM-It was not until the 1991 Gulf War that modern Americans could appreciate the dread of chemical warfare. This knowledge brings Marine Gunnery Sergeant Stockham's deed more into perspective. He received his Medal of Honor for giving his gas mask to a wounded comrade during a German gas attack in Belleau Wood, France, on June 14, 1918. Stockham died nine days later.

Stockham's Medal of Honor was awarded 21 years later by President Franklin Delano Roosevelt. Marine Colonel Clifton Cates, who had been a Second Lieutenant at Belleau Wood, called Stockham "the bravest man I ever knew." After World War II, Cates rose to become Commandant of the Marine Corps. None of Stockham's family lived to receive his Medal.

FREDDIE STOWERS-Corporal Stowers of the segregated 93rd Infantry Division was killed in France on September 28, 1918, when he and other soldiers were receiving the surrender of German troops who then opened fire on them.

No black servicemen were honored with the Medal of Honor for World War I service until President George Bush awarded this Medal on April 24, 1991, more than 72 years after the action for which it was awarded.

RALPH TALBOT-Second Lieutenant Talbot became the first Marine airman to be awarded the Medal of Honor and the only one during World War I. His medal was for two separate missions in which he shot down three German planes. Although he survived these actions, the Medal was awarded posthumously when he died after crashing on takeoff on October 25, 1918. His observer, Second Lieutenant Colgate W. Darden Jr., survived the crash, later becoming Governor of Virginia and President of the University of Virginia.

CHARLES W. WHITTLESEY-Major Whittlesey was the commander of the "Lost Battalion" that was surrounded and cut off for five days by German forces in the Argonne Forest in October of 1918. Refusing German surrender demands, his battalion suffered 70 percent casualties before their rescue.

After the war, Whittlesey was chosen by General John J. Pershing as one of three Medal of Honor recipients to act as pallbearers for the Unknown Soldier of World War I. The other two were First Lieutenant Samuel Woodfill of the 5th Infantry Division and Sergeant Alvin C. York of the 82nd Infantry Division. Whittlesey committed suicide while at sea between New York and Cuba in November of 1921. His body was not recovered.

ALVIN C. YORK-Corporal York, later to become the famous "Sergeant York" after Gary Cooper portrayed him in a 1941 motion picture, received his Medal of Honor for actions on October 8, 1918, that resulted in capturing over 130 German soldiers. He was also the only enlisted man to serve as a pallbearer for the Unknown Soldier of World War I. His postwar fame led people to assume he was the most highly decorated American serviceman of the war but he was not. Exclusive of the five Marines who earned double awards of the Medal, Lt. Samuel Parker was the most highly decorated soldier of World War I.

When World War II started, York attempted to re-enlist at the age of 55 but was rejected due to his age. He died on September 2, 1964, at the age of 76.

HAITIAN CAMPAIGN
1919-1920

MARINE CORPS-2 awards to 2 individuals, both new recipients, neither posthumous.

TOTAL-2 awards to 2 individuals, both new recipients, neither posthumous.

Revolutionary resistance rose anew in Haiti in late 1919. Two Medals of Honor were awarded to Marines for the same action on October 31-November 1, 1919. Oddly enough, both men were from St. Louis, Missouri.

BY RANK:

MARINES

2nd Lieutenant	1
Corporal	1

AGE OF RECIPIENTS:

20-29	2

AVERAGE AGE: 25

YOUNGEST RECIPIENT:

Marine Corporal William Robert Button, born December 3, 1895, was 24 when he earned his Medal on July 1, 1920. (see below)

OLDEST RECIPIENT:

Marine Second Lieutenant Herman Henry Hanneken, born June 23, 1893, was 27 when he earned his Medal on July 1, 1920. (see below)

NOTABLE INDIVIDUALS:

WILLIAM ROBERT BUTTON-Marine Corporal Button was awarded his Medal of Honor for the same action as Herman Hanneken (below), in which the two men killed a rebel leader while heavily outnumbered. Although he survived the action, Button died from malaria on April 15, 1921, and did not live to receive his Medal.

HERMAN HENRY HANNEKEN-Hanneken was a Marine Sergeant at the time of the action for which he received his Medal of Honor. He received the Navy Cross for killing another rebel leader in Haiti the following April. Commissioned as an officer in 1920, he also fought in Nicaragua, won a Silver Star as a Lieutenant Colonel on Guadalcanal in 1942, was a Colonel on Peleliu in 1943 and retired as a Brigadier General in 1948. Widely known by his nicknames of "Hard Head" and "Haiti" Hanneken, he was described as "silent and cold-eyed." He died on August 23, 1986, at the age of 93.

Second Nicaraguan Campaign
1928-1932

MARINE CORPS-2 awards to 2 individuals, both new recipients, neither posthumous.

TOTAL-2 awards to 2 individuals, both new recipients, neither posthumous.

Civil War erupted in Nicaragua in 1925. A Marine Brigade and a Marine Aviation Squadron supported the efforts of the Nicaraguan National Guard for the next several years until order was restored.

Two Medals of Honor were awarded for actions in 1928 and 1932. The awards were given to one officer in the Aviation Squadron and one enlisted man in the ground forces.

BY RANK:

MARINES

1st Lieutenant	1
Corporal	1

AGE OF RECIPIENTS:

30-39	1
20-29	1

AVERAGE AGE: 28

YOUNGEST RECIPIENT:

Marine Corporal Donald Leroy Truesdell, born August 8, 1906, was 25 when he earned his Medal on April 24, 1932.

OLDEST RECIPIENT:

Marine First Lieutenant Christian Franklin Schilt, born March

18, 1895, was 32 when he earned his Medal on January 6-8, 1928. (See below)

NOTABLE INDIVIDUALS:

CHRISTIAN FRANK SCHILT-First Lieutenant Schilt became the second Marine airman to win a Medal of Honor by flying ten missions to evacuate wounded and bring in supplies on January 6-8, 1928. Schilt later rose to become a four-star general and the Commander of Marine Aviation.

NON-COMBAT ACTIONS
1920-1940

ARMY-2 awards to 2 individuals, both new recipients, neither posthumous.

NAVY-15 awards to 15 individuals, all new recipients, 4 posthumous.

MARINE CORPS-1 award to 1 individual, new recipient, not posthumous.

TOTAL-18 awards to 18 individuals, all new recipients, 4 posthumous.

The Army made two awards during this period. One was for career service to 90-year old Major General Adolphus Greeley who had been retired for 30 years. The other was to Army Air Corps Reserve Captain Charles Lindbergh for his solo flight across the Atlantic in 1927.

Of the 15 Navy awards:
1 was to Richard Byrd for his flight over the North Pole.
2 (posthumously) were to crashed airmen.
4 were given during the sinking of the submarine *Squalus*.
2 (both posthumous) were given for a fire on the U.S.S. *Trenton*.

BY RANK:

ARMY		NAVY		MARINES	
Major General	1	Commander	1	Private	1
Captain	1	Lt. Commander	2 (1)		
		Lieutenant	1 (1)		
		Ensign	2 (1)		
		Boatswains Mate 1/c	1 (1)		
		Chief Boatswains Mte	1		

Chief Gunners Mate   1
Chief Machinists Mte   1
Chief Metalsmith   1
Machinist   1
Machinists Mate   1
Torpedoman 1/c   1
Torpedoman 2/c   1

BY LOCATION OF ACTION:

Unknown	7
North Pole	2
Atlantic Ocean	2
Pacific Ocean	1
Connecticut	1
Florida	1
Virginia	1
General Service	1
Sea of Marmora	1
Japan	1

AGE OF RECIPIENTS:

40-49	2
30-39	7
20-29	8
Retiree	1

AVERAGE AGE: 30
(Not counting General Greeley. See below)

YOUNGEST RECIPIENT:

Navy Ensign Thomas John Ryan Jr., born August 5, 1901, was 22 when he earned his Medal for rescuing a woman from a burning hotel in Yokohama, Japan, on September 1, 1923. He died seven months later.

OLDEST RECIPIENT:

Army major General Adolphus Washington Greeley was born on March 27, 1844. Enlisting as a Private at the age of 17 on July 26, 1861, he advanced to the rank of Major General by the time he retired on his 64th birthday (as was the law at that time) in 1908. His Medal of Honor was awarded for his entire career of service by special legislation of Congress on March 27, 1935, on his 91st birthday. He died seven months later.

His Medal was the second non-combat award for an entire career of general service.

NOTABLE INDIVIDUALS:

HENRY BREAULT-Torpedoman Second Class Breault was awarded the Medal of Honor for actions on October 28, 1923. On that date, the U.S. submarine *O-5* collided with a steamship and sank in less than a minute. Breault could have safely left the vessel but returned to save a trapped shipmate, becoming trapped in the sinking sub himself. He was rescued by divers 31 hours later. Submariners would not be awarded Medals of Honor for combat actions until World War II but Breault became the first submariner to earn one.

UNKNOWN SOLDIERS

ARMY-9 awards of the Army Medal of Honor to 9 unknown individuals, all posthumous.

TOTAL-9 awards of the Army Medal of Honor to 9 unknown individuals, 5 to foreign nationals, all posthumous.

The original Tomb of the Unknown Soldier was created in Arlington National Cemetery to honor all of the unknown dead servicemen following The Great War or, as it was also known, The War To End All Wars. The name was created to personify the horrible carnage of that war and a future conflict of even greater magnitude could not be envisioned by the people of that day. It didn't become World War I until December 7, 1941.

On Memorial Day, 1921, four unidentified bodies were exhumed from military cemeteries in France. One was selected as The Unknown Soldier and the other three were re-buried in the Meuse Argonne Cemetery in France.

On Armistice Day, November 11, 1921, The Unknown Soldier was interred in Arlington National Cemetery after having a Medal of Honor pinned to the flag covering his coffin by President Warren Harding. The ceremony was also attended by dignitaries from the allied nations of Great Britain, France, Belgium, Italy and Rumania. Each of those nations conferred their country's highest military decoration upon The Unknown Soldier and President Harding awarded a Medal of Honor to the Unknown Soldier of each of those nations. Congress and the President officially authorized these presentations to the Unknown Soldiers of the following nations on the following dates:

Great Britain and France	March 4, 1921
United States	August 24, 1921
Italy	October 12, 1921
Belgium	December 1, 1922
Rumania	June 6, 1923

Thus the Medal of Honor was officially approved for the Unknown Soldiers of Great Britain and France more than five months before one was authorized for the Unknown Soldier of World War I from America.

Following World War II, two unidentified bodies were exhumed, one each from the Pacific and European theaters of action. Placed in identical caskets, they were taken off the coast of Virginia on the USS *Canberra*. One was selected as The Unknown Soldier of World War II. The other one was buried at sea with full military honors. Congress authorized the award of the Medal of Honor to the Unknown Soldier of World War II on March 9, 1948. After the Korean War, four unidentified bodies from that conflict were exhumed from the National Memorial Cemetery of the Pacific in Honolulu, Hawaii. One was selected as The Unknown Soldier of the Korean War and Congress authorized the award of the Medal of Honor on August 31, 1957.

On May 28, 1958, the Unknown Soldiers of World War II and Korea were taken to Washington, D.C., and lay in state in the Capitol rotunda until Memorial Day. On that day, they were both interred in Arlington National Cemetery after being awarded the Medal of Honor by President Dwight Eisenhower. That area of Arlington was officially renamed The Tomb of the Unknowns.

A fourth Unknown Soldier, this time from the Vietnam War, was interred at Arlington on May 28, 1984, after being awarded the Medal of Honor by President Ronald Reagan. The delay was due to advanced medical techniques for identifying bodies. Identification techniques, primarily involving DNA analysis, have advanced to the point where almost <u>any</u> portion of recovered remains, no matter how small, can be identified.

In fact, modern science has made the Unknown Soldier of Vietnam a situation currently in limbo. News reports on January 20, 1998, indicated that the person buried as the Vietnam Unknown Soldier was "almost certainly" an Air Force pilot named Michael Joseph Blassie who was 24 years old when he was shot down near An Loc in May of 1972. The following October, a ground patrol found skeletal remains, a shredded flight suit and Blassie's identity card. The remains were formally designated as "believed to be" those of Blassie. They were provided to Arlington Cemetery in 1980 after increasing pressure from the Pentagon to add a Vietnam serviceman's body to the Tomb of the Unknowns.

The remains were exhumed and, in June of 1998, were positively identified as those of First Lieutenant Blassie and he was reburied in St. Louis, Missouri.

That Medal of Honor is still counted in these statistics. As of July of 1998, there are still 2,124 American servicemen listed as Missing In Action from the Vietnam War. Although that Medal no longer belongs to Lt. Blassie, it should belong to one of those men...for all of them.

Awards of the Medal of Honor require documentation by at least two witnesses to the acts that are honored. Obviously this is not always possible and these untold thousands of unknown acts of heroism are what the awards to the Unknown Soldiers are intended to honor. I can think of no better example of this than one included in Stephen Ambrose's book *D-Day, June 6, 1944, The Climactic Battle of World War II* (Simon and Schuster, New York, NY, 1994). It is an excerpt from an oral history collected at the Eisenhower Center at the University of New Orleans. Near dawn on June 6, 1944, Private John Fitzgerald of the 101st Airborne Division, far from his intended drop zone, made his way into Ste.-Mere-Eglise, France. The trees were draped with dead American paratroopers, shot while hanging helplessly in their chutes. Nearby, he saw a sight he would never forget.

"It was a picture story of the death of one 82nd Airborne trooper. He had occupied a German foxhole and made it his personal Alamo. In a half circle around the hole lay the bodies of nine German soldiers. The body closest to the hole was only three feet away, a potato masher [grenade] in his fist. The other distorted forms lay where they had fallen, testimony to the ferocity of the fight. His ammunition bandoliers were still on his shoulders, empty of M-1 clips. Cartridge cases littered the ground. His rifle stock was broken in two. He had fought alone and, like many others that night, died alone.

I looked at his dogtags. The name read Martin V. Hersh. I wrote the name down in a small prayer book I carried, hoping someday I would meet someone who knew him. I never did."

Thus it is only through the happenstance of war that the name of Martin V. Hersh is not included among these honored heroes. Nevertheless, his story tells us something. There are thousands of stories like his that we don't know and no one will ever know. The "Unknown" in the title of the Unknown Soldiers refers to much more than their identities and their Medals of Honor belong to many others that do not rest in their hallowed tomb.

WORLD WAR II
1941-1945

ARMY-324 awards to 324 individuals, all new recipients, 266 posthumous.

NAVY-57 awards to 57 individuals, all new recipients, 32 posthumous.

MARINE CORPS-82 awards to 82 individuals, all new recipients, 51 posthumous.

COAST GUARD-1 award to 1 individual, new recipient, posthumous.

TOTAL-464 awards to 464 individuals, all new recipients, 266 posthumous.

Just as the U.S. had gained a belated entry into the First World War, so it would in the biggest conflict in the history of the world. Europe was set ablaze in September of 1939 but the war didn't start for America until Pearl Harbor was attacked on December 7, 1941.

As it was in its infancy in World War I, the Air Corps was a branch of the Army while the Navy and Marines had their own separate air arms.

The Army put the majority of its efforts, ground and air, into the European Theater from the beginning. Ground combat in the Pacific Theater, the infamous island-hopping campaign, was left primarily to the Marine Corps. The Navy battled worldwide.

BY RANK:
(Posthumous awards in parentheses)

ARMY			NAVY		
General	2		Rear Admiral	3	(3)
Brig. Gen	4	(3)	Captain	4	(4)
Colonel	5	(1)	Commander	13	(4)
Lt. Col.	6	(4)	Lt. Commander	3	(1)
Major	10	(5)	Lieutenant	7	(2)

Rank	Count		Rank	Count
Captain	13 (9)		Lieutenant j.g.	4 (1)
1st Lt.	36 16)		Ensign	3 (3)
2nd Lt.	24 (18)		Boatswains Mte 1/c	1 (1)
Flight Ofr	1		Boatswains Mte 2/c	1 (1)
First Sgt.	2 (1)		Chief Boatswain	1 (1)
Master Sgt.	3		Gunner	1
Staff Sgt.	41 (21)		Chief Watertender	2 (2)
Tech. Sgt.	24 (6)		Hospital Appr 1/c	2 (1)
Sergeant	33 (20)		Warrant Machinist	1
Tech. 5th Gd	6 (5)		Machinists Mate 1/c	1 (1)
Tech. 4th Gd.	2 (2)		Pharmacists Mate 1/c	2 (1)
Corporal	12 (5)		Pharmacists Mate 2/c	2 (1)
PFC	61 (41)		Pharmacists Mate 3/c	1 (1)
Private	39 (25)		Radio Electrician	1 (1)
			Seaman 1/c	2 (2)
			Watertender 1/c	1 (1)
			Aviation Chf. Ord	1

MARINES

Rank	Count
Major General	1
Colonel	2
Lt. Col.	3 (2)
Major	5 (2)
Captain	8 (2)
1st Lt.	10 (7)
2nd Lt.	1
Gunnery Sgt.	2 (2)
Staff Sgt.	3 (2)
Sergeant	9 (7)
Corporal	10 (6)
PFC	20 (16)
Private	8 (5)

COAST GUARD

Rank	Count
Signalman	1 (1)

TOTALS:

ARMY	324 (182)
NAVY	57 (32)
MARINES	82 (51)
COAST GUARD	1 (1)

BY LOCATION OF ACTION:

EUROPEAN THEATER

France	71
Italy	68
Germany	56
Belgium	18
Rumania	7
Sicily	5
Over Europe	5
Holland	3
Morocco	3
Tunisia	3
Luxembourg	2
Atlantic Ocean	1
Multiple areas	1

PACIFIC THEATER

Philippine Islands	49
Iwo Jima	27
Okinawa	24
Pacific Ocean	17
Hawaii	16
Solomon Islands	15
New Guinea	11
Guadalcanal	10
Peleliu	8
Saipan	7
Bougainville	5
Guam	4
Savo Island	4
Tarawa	4
Namur Island	3
New Britain	3
Tinian	2
Over Japan	2
Midway Island	2
Attu	1
Burma	1
Eniwetok	1
Los Negros Island	1
Makin Island	1
Neth'lnds E.Indies	1
Roi Island	1
South China Sea	1
Truk Island	1
Wake Island	1

TOTAL	**241**	**223**

MOST DECORATED UNITS:

ARMY (DIVISION LEVEL)

3rd Infantry Division	36
1st Infantry Division	16
36th Infantry Division	13
32nd Infantry Division	11
45th Infantry Division	8

REGIMENTAL LEVEL

442nd Regimental Combat Team	21
15th Infantry, 3rd Division	15
18th Infantry, 1st Division	8
30th Infantry, 3rd Division	7
142nd Infantry, 36th Division	6
127th Infantry, 32nd Division	6

COMPANY LEVEL

Co. I, 15th Inf., 3rd Division	3
Co. K, 18th Inf., 1st Division	3
Co. B, 15th Inf., 3rd Division	2
Co. E, 142nd Inf., 36th Division	2

MARINES (DIVISION LEVEL)

1st Marine Division	14
5th Marine Division	14
4th Marine Division	10
3rd Marine Division	8
2nd Marine Division	6
6th Marine Division	6

REGIMENTAL LEVEL

1st Reg., 1st Marines	6
7th Reg., 1st Marines	4
27th Reg., 5th Marines	4

28th Reg., 5th Marines   4

COMPANY LEVEL

Co. C, 1st Reg., 1st Marines   3

MARINES

(BY BATTLE)

Iwo Jima	23	(not including 5 awards to the Army and Navy)
Okinawa	10	(not including 12 awards to the Army and Navy.)
Air battles	10	
Guadalcanal	9	(not including 4 awards to: Army Navy & Cst Grd)
Peleliu	8	
Kwajalein	4	
Saipan	4	(not including 3 awards to the Army and Navy.)
Tarawa	4	
Guam	4	
Bougainville	4	(not including 1 award to the Army.)

NAVY

(BY BATTLE)		(BY SHIP)	
Pearl Harbor	15 (11)	U.S.S. *California*	4
Kaneohe Air Sta.	1	U.S.S. *Arizona*	3
Submarines	7 (3)	U.S.S. *Nevada*	2
Air battles	6	U.S.S. *Oklahoma*	2
PT Boats	2	U.S.S. *Utah*	1
		U.S.S. *Vestal*	1
		U.S.S. *West Virginia*	1

BY SHIP TYPE

Battleships	13
Aircraft Carrier	3
Cruisers	8
Destroyers	2
Minesweepers	1

ARMY AIR CORPS:

The Army Air Corps was a part of the U.S. Army during World War II as it had been during the first world war. Successively named the Army Air Corps and then the Army Air Forces, it was finally granted status as a separate service in September of 1947. The statistics for Medal of Honor recipients for this service are included under the Army in other tables. The specific World War II totals for the Air Corps alone are as follows:

UNIT

	Posthumous	Total
8th Air Force	10	15
5th Air Force	6	10
9th Air Force	3	6
Headquarters, AAC	1	3
12th Air Force	1	1
14th Air Force	1	1
15th Air Force	1	1
20th Air Force	0	1
TOTALS	**23**	**38**

BLACK RECIPIENTS:

World War II was the last conflict in which the American military was segregated. Although black servicemen were awarded medals for valor, none received the Medal of Honor. On January 13, 1997, President Bill Clinton awarded Medals of Honor to seven black men for World War II actions.

They were:

2nd Lieutenant Vernon J. Baker, 92nd Infantry Division, for actions in Italy on April 5-6, 1945.

Staff Sergeant Edward A. Carter, 12th Armored Division, for actions in Germany, March 23, 1945.

1st Lieutenant John R. Fox, 92nd Infantry Division, for actions in Italy, December 26, 1944.

PFC Willy F. James Jr., 104th Infantry Division, for actions in Germany, April 7, 1945.

Staff Sergeant Ruben Rivers, 761st Tank Battalion, for actions in France, November 15-19, 1944.

1st Lieutenant Charles L. Thomas, 103rd Infantry Division, for actions in France, December 14, 1944.

Private George Watson, 29th Quartermaster Regiment, for actions at sea off the coast of New Guinea, March 8, 1943.

Six of the awards were posthumous. Four were killed in action and although Thomas and Carter survived the war, they died before receiving their awards. Baker was the only one who lived to receive his award. The most highly decorated black soldier in the European Theater, Baker, 77, was retired from the Army and had already received the Distinguished Service Cross, Bronze Star, Purple Heart, Polish Cross of Valor and Italian Cross of Valor. Carter, Fox, James and Thomas had previously been awarded the DSC and Rivers the Silver Star. Based upon the monthly tax-free stipend legislated for Medal of Honor recipients, Baker was awarded $64,000 in back pay.

ASIA-PACIFIC AMERICAN RECIPIENTS:

Only two Asia-Pacific Americans received Medals of Honor during World War II. This was rectified on June 21, 2000, when 22 World War II veterans of this ethnicity were awarded Medals of Honor. One of the awards was an upgrade from an original award of the Silver Star and the remainder were upgrades of the Distinguished Service Cross. A complete list is included at the end of the book.

AGE OF RECIPIENTS:

60-69	1
50-59	10
40-49	22

30-39	62
20-29	293
Age 19	21
Age 18	4
Age 17	1
Unknown	50
AVERAGE AGE:	26

YOUNGEST RECIPIENT:

Marine Private First Class Jacklyn Harold Lucas, born on February 14, 1928, enlisted at 14 by forging his mother's signature. He was only six days past his 17th birthday when he earned his Medal on Iwo Jima on February 20, 1945. See under Notable Individuals.

OLDEST RECIPIENT:

General Douglas MacArthur, born January 26, 1880, was 62 when he earned his Medal for his defense of the Philippine Islands in early 1942. His award also makes him the oldest of all recipients at the time of the Medal action.

NOTABLE INDIVIDUALS:

RICHARD NOTT ANTRIM-Navy Commander Antrim (then Lieutenant) was awarded the Medal of Honor for his actions as a prisoner of war in the Netherlands East Indies in April of 1942. He became the only recipient who earned his Medal while a POW in that war. Surviving the war, he rose to the rank of Rear Admiral, retired in 1954 and died on March 8, 1969.

JOHN BASILONE-Marine Sergeant Basilone earned his Medal of Honor during a Japanese banzai attack on Guadalcanal on October 24-25, 1942. Turning down a commission as an officer, he went on a stateside tour to sell war bonds. Although he could have stayed out of combat, he requested a return to a combat unit. He was killed on Iwo Jima in February of 1945 and was posthumously awarded the Navy Cross.

HAROLD WILLIAM BAUER-Marine Lieutenant Colonel Bauer was awarded his Medal of Honor for shooting down 11 Japanese planes in the Pacific Theater between May and November of 1942. An Annapolis graduate, Bauer had been the quarterback of the Naval Academy's football team in 1930. Bauer was shot down and lost at sea on November 14, 1942, before he received his Medal of Honor.

EDWARD A. BENNETT-Corporal Bennett of the Army's 90th Infantry Division was awarded his Medal of Honor for actions in Germany on February 1, 1945. He had been drafted in January of 1944 and also earned the Silver Star, Bronze Star and four Purple Hearts. He was commissioned as an officer in June of 1951 and served in Korea. Retiring after a heart attack at the age of 42 in October of 1962, he died on May 2, 1983.

WILLIBALD C. BIANCHI-First Lieutenant Bianchi was awarded the Medal of Honor for his actions during the defense of Bataan in the Philippines in February of 1942. Captured, he survived the Bataan Death march and two years as a prisoner of war of the Japanese. Bianchi was killed in December of 1944 when he was one of a group of American POW's being taken to Japan on a Japanese freighter that was attacked and sunk by American planes.

RICHARD I. BONG-Army Air Corps Major Bong was the highest scoring ace of World War II, shooting down 40 Japanese planes. After receiving his Medal of Honor, he became a test pilot and was killed in the crash of an experimental P-80 jet fighter on August 6, 1945, the same day the first atomic bomb was dropped on Japan.

GREGORY BOYINGTON-Marine Major Boyington became the first American ace of World War II. He earned that status as a member of the American Volunteer Group (The Flying Tigers) before America even entered the war. Including the 6 Japanese planes he shot down as a Flying Tiger, Boyington ended the war with a total of 28 kills, the most of any Marine airman. He died on January 11, 1988, in Fresno, California, at the age of 75.

MAURICE L. BRITT-Captain Britt of the Army's 3rd Infantry Division became the first American soldier of World War II to win the nation's top three medals. He was awarded the Silver Star in September of 1943, the Medal of Honor in November of 1943 and the Distinguished Service Cross in January of 1944. He also received the Bronze Star, two Purple Hearts and the British Military Cross. Audie Murphy eventually surpassed his total and he ended the war as the second most highly decorated American serviceman. A former football star for the University of Arkansas and an end for the NFL's Detroit Lions pro football team, Britt was 6'3" tall, weighed 220 pounds and wore a size 13 1/2 shoe. He had his right arm amputated as a result of his wounds and later became Arkansas' first Republican Attorney General since Reconstruction.

BOBBIE E. BROWN-Captain Brown was awarded his Medal of Honor for actions with the 1st Infantry Division at Aachen, Germany, on October 8, 1944. Having joined the Army at the age of 15 at the end of World War I, Brown also received two Silver Stars, a Bronze Star and was wounded 13 times. After the war, he became a janitor at West Point. He committed suicide on November 12, 1971, at the age of 68.

JOSE CALUGAS-Sergeant Calugas was awarded his Medal of Honor for his actions in the defense of Bataan on January 16, 1942. After surviving the Bataan Death March, he remained a POW throughout the war. Repatriated to the Army after victory, he retired as a Captain in 1957. Calugas was the second Asian-Pacific American to be awarded the Medal of Honor and the first since 1911.

HORACE S. CARSWELL JR.-Major Carswell was posthumously awarded the Medal of Honor when he was killed piloting a B-24 bomber against a convoy of Japanese ships in the South China Sea on October 26, 1944. When the plane was damaged beyond hope, Carswell ordered the enlisted men to bail out, leaving himself and two Lieutenants on board. One of the Lieutenants' parachutes had been shredded by gunfire, leaving only two chutes between the three officers. All three died when the plane crashed, two of whom could have saved themselves but chose not to at that price. Carswell Air Force Base in his hometown of Fort Worth, Texas, is named for him.

ANTHONY CASAMENTO-Marine Corporal Casamento, Company D, 1st Battalion, 5th Marines, 1st Marine Division, was seriously wounded while leading a machine gun section against Japanese on Guadalcanal on November 1, 1942. President Jimmy Carter belatedly presented his Medal to him on September 12, 1980.

FREDERICK W. CASTLE-Brigadier General Castle was commanding a force of over 2,000 bombers against German airfields on Christmas Eve of 1944. When his bomber was shot up too badly to complete the mission, General Castle ordered the crew to bail out and remained at the controls alone so they could escape. He was posthumously awarded the Medal of Honor and Castle Air Force Base in Merced, California, was later named for him.

ERNEST L. CHILDERS-Second Lieutenant Childers was awarded his Medal of Honor for actions in Italy with the 45th Infantry Division on September 22, 1943. Childers had joined the Oklahoma National Guard (45th Infantry) in 1937. He also served in Korea and retired as a Colonel in 1966. A Creek Indian, Childers was the first Native American to be awarded the Medal of Honor since the Indian Campaigns of the previous century.

Although no statistics on Medals awarded to graduates of the same school exist, Lt. Childers and First Lt. Jack Montgomery (also of the 45th Division) both graduated from the Chilocco Indian Agriculture School in Chilocco, Oklahoma. This is almost certainly the smallest school to produce two Medal of Honor recipients.

RAYMOND H. COOLEY-Staff Sergeant Cooley of the Army's 25th Infantry Division was awarded the Medal of Honor for his actions in the Philippines on February 24, 1945. He lost his right hand from wounds he received when a grenade exploded in his hand. After the war, he became an alcoholic and was killed in a car wreck while intoxicated on March 12, 1947.

WILLIAM J. CRAWFORD-Private Crawford of the Army's 36th Infantry Division was awarded the Medal of Honor for his actions in Italy on September 13, 1943. His Medal was originally given to his father in 1944 when he was missing in action and presumed dead. He was, in fact, a German POW. After the war he claimed his Medal but no formal presentation was made. He retired from the Army as a Master Sergeant. On May 30, 1984, President Reagan formally presented Crawford's Medal to him at graduation ceremonies at the U.S. Air Force Academy where he was working as a custodian.

MICHAEL J. DALY-At the beginning of World War II, Daly resigned from West Point after his freshman year to enlist in the Army as a Private. He earned a battlefield commission, two Silver Stars and, on April 18, 1945, the Medal of Honor. His father had won a Distinguished Service Cross in World War I, volunteered for World War II, served on Guadalcanal, was wounded in France and was being evacuated to the U.S. at about the same time his son was earning the nation's highest honor.

JAMES L. DAY-As a 19-year-old squad leader on Okinawa, Corporal Day, 2nd Battalion, 22nd Marines, 6th Marine Division, repelled several Japanese attacks on Sugar Loaf Hill as well as dragging five wounded comrades to safety between May 14-17, 1945. When finally relieved on the third day, more than 100 enemy dead were around his position.

Day remained in the Marines and is believed to be the only Marine to serve as an infantryman, be wounded and decorated for valor in World War II, Korea and Vietnam. For years he forbade his men for recommending him for a decoration for the Okinawa action while he was still on active duty. In the interim he had earned the Distinguished Service Medal, three Silver Stars, the Legion of Merit for Valor, the Bronze Star for Valor, two Navy Commendation Medals for Valor, six Purple Hearts and over 25 other awards. After retiring as a Major General in 1986, he was awarded the Medal of Honor on January 20, 1998, by President Bill Clinton. He died on October 28, 1998.

SAMUEL DAVID DEALEY-In five patrols, Navy Commander Dealey's submarine, the U.S.S. *Harder*, sank 15 Japanese ships totaling 54,000 tons. He was awarded the Medal of Honor after his submarine was sunk in action off the coast of the Philippines on August 24, 1944. Dealey Plaza (where President John F. Kennedy was assassinated in 1963) in his hometown of Dallas, Texas, was named in his honor.

JEFFERSON JOSEPH DeBLANC-Marine pilot Captain DeBlanc finished the war with 9 confirmed kills and 3 probables. He retired from the Marine Corps as a Colonel in 1972. Earning a Ph.D. degree, he taught mathematics, physics and computer science at Southwest Louisiana Institute.

DESMOND T. DOSS-Private First Class Doss earned his Medal of Honor saving others as a Medic on Okinawa. He was the first conscientious objector to win the nation's highest honor.

ROBERT H. DUNLAP-Marine Captain Dunlap earned the Medal of Honor on Iwo Jima on the same day one of the men in his company, Jacklyn Lucas, became the youngest Marine to ever win the Medal. Dunlap's cousin, Navy Captain James B. Stockdale, earned the Medal of Honor as a POW in the Vietnam War, the only known instance in which cousins earned the Medal.

MERRITT AUSTIN EDSON-Colonel Edson was awarded his Medal of Honor while serving as the commander of the famous 1st Marine Raider Battalion (Edson's Raiders) on Guadalcanal in September of 1942. He finished his career as a Major General having also won two Navy Crosses, two Legion of Merit medals and the Silver Star. He committed suicide on August 14, 1955.

WALTER D. EHLERS-Staff Sergeant Ehlers of the 1st Infantry Division was awarded the Medal of Honor for his actions immediately following D-Day in June of 1944. Ehlers had joined the Army with his brother who was killed on D-Day. He also won the Silver Star, two Bronze Stars and four Purple Hearts. He worked for the Veterans Administration after the war. On the 50th anniversary of

D-Day, June 6, 1994, Ehlers and President Bill Clinton placed a wreath at the U.S. Cemetery in Normandy.

HENRY E. ERWIN-Staff Sergeant Erwin was one of the rarest Medal of Honor recipients, an enlisted man in the Army Air Corps. Serving as a radioman on a B-29 in a bombing raid over Japan on April 12, 1945, Erwin was dropping phosphorus flares when a faulty one exploded in his face, burning his nose off and blinding him. Enveloped in flame, he crawled to a window and threw the flare out, saving the plane.

He was recommended for the Medal of Honor and, because it was considered that he would certainly not survive, it was approved in only six days. Since no Medal of Honor was available, a plane was sent to Hawaii where one was on display and it was returned and awarded to him.

Against all odds, Erwin survived but he had 41 plastic surgeries for his wounds. After the war, he went to work for the Veterans Administration.

RICHARD E. FLEMING-Marine Captain Fleming posthumously received the only Medal of Honor awarded for the battle of Midway in June of 1942. He was killed in the last of a series of bombing attacks against Japanese warships. The airport in his hometown of St. Paul, Minnesota, is named in his honor.

EUGENE BENNETT FLUCKEY-Commanding the U.S.S. *Barb*, Commander Fluckey was the second-highest scoring submarine commander of World War II. Also winning four Navy Crosses, he retired as a Rear Admiral.

JOSEPH JACOB FOSS-Captain Foss became the second-highest scoring Marine ace of the war with 26 kills, tying Eddie Rickenbacker's World War I record. Retiring from the Air National Guard as a Brigadier General, he later became the Governor of South Dakota, Commissioner of the American Football League and President of the National Rifle Association.

LEONARD A. FUNK JR.-A First Sergeant with the 82nd Airborne

Division, Funk became the most decorated paratrooper of World War II. In addition to his Medal of Honor for action in Belgium in January of 1945, he also won the Distinguished Service Cross, Silver Star, Bronze Star and three Purple Hearts. He retired from the Veterans Administration in 1972 after 25 years of service.

HOWARD WALTER GILMORE-On February 7, 1943, Commander Gilmore became the first submariner to win the Medal of Honor in combat. The commander of the U.S.S. *Growler* when they rammed a Japanese gunboat, Gilmore ordered the bridge cleared. Wounded by machine gun bullets and unable to save himself, he ordered the submarine to submerge while he was still topside.

DONALD J. GOTT-WILLIAM E. METZGER-First Lieutenant Gott and Second Lieutenant Metzger were pilot and co-pilot on a B-17 badly shot up over Saarbrucken, Germany, on November 9, 1944. Ordering the rest of the crew to bail out, both officers refused to leave the crippled plane in an attempt to save a wounded crewman. Both were killed when the plane exploded in flight over France. Both officers were posthumously awarded the Medal of Honor.

A memorial tombstone was placed over an empty grave in Gott's hometown of Arnett, Oklahoma. Aided by witnesses accounts almost half a century later, on August 16, 1994, Gott's and Metzger's bodies were identified in an unmarked grave in France. This is the only known case where two Medal of Honor recipients were buried in the same grave.

GEORGE J. HALL-Staff Sergeant Hall of the 34th Infantry Division was awarded the Medal of Honor for single-handedly attacking 3 German machine gun nests near Anzio, Italy, on May 23, 1944. After knocking out two of the nests, his right leg was partially severed by an artillery shellburst. Hall amputated his own leg and eventually succumbed to his wounds on February 16, 1946.

PIERPONT M. HAMILTON-Army Air Corps Major Hamilton was awarded his Medal of Honor for his participation in a mission during the invasion of North Africa on November 8, 1942. While trying to prevent Vichy French resistance, they came under fire and one of his colleagues was killed. Hamilton was a direct descendant of Alexander Hamilton. He retired from the Air Force as a Major General in 1952 and died on March 4, 1982.

ROBERT MURRAY HANSON-First Lieutenant Hanson's success in war came about so fast that the press didn't have time to make him famous before his death. Nicknamed "Butcher Bob" in VMF-215, he shot down 20 Japanese planes in 17 days, becoming the Marine Corps' third-highest ranking ace. He was shot down and killed by ground fire on Rabaul on February 3, 1944, the day before his 24th birthday.

WILLIAM GEORGE HARRELL-Marine Sergeant Harrell was attacked by a Japanese suicide squad on Iwo Jima on March 3, 1945. He killed several of them until his left hand was blown off by a grenade. Attacked by others, he also killed them with a pistol until the last one threw a grenade near him. Picking up the grenade with his remaining hand, he thrust it into the chest of the last enemy soldier, killing the enemy and blowing off his other hand.

After the war, he was fitted with prosthetic hooks to replace his hands and became very proficient with them. He designed a device that allowed him to use firearms accurately and became the head of the prosthetics group of the Veterans Administration working with amputee veterans like himself. Later in life, Harrell became involved in a love triangle and on August 9, 1964, he committed suicide after killing a neighbor and the neighbor's wife.

SILVESTRE SANTANA HERRERA-Private First Class Herrera earned his Medal of Honor on March 15, 1945, while serving with the Army's 36th Infantry Division near Merzwiller, France. With his unit pinned down by German machine gun fire, Herrera knowingly attacked the Germans through a minefield. He continued fighting even after a landmine had blown off both of his feet.

PFC Herrera had been born in Mexico. A year after being awarded his Medal of Honor, Mexico awarded him its highest medal for valor, the *Premier Merito Militar*. Thus far, he is the only person authorized to wear the highest military awards of both the United States and Mexico.

JAMES A. HOWARD-A former Navy pilot, Howard shot down 6 Japanese fighters while a member of the Flying Tigers. Joining the Army Air Corps after America's entry into the war, he fought with the 8th Air Force in Europe. On January 11, 1944, Lieutenant Colonel Howard was flying fighter cover for a bombing raid when he single-handedly attacked a flight of 30 German fighters, shooting down three of them. He was the only fighter pilot in the European Theater to receive the Medal of Honor. He retired from the Air Force as a Brigadier General.

LEON W. JOHNSON-Army Air Corps Colonel Johnson was awarded his Medal of Honor for his actions as a bomber pilot raiding the Ploesti oil fields in Rumania on August 1, 1943. Retiring from the Air Force as a four-star General, he died in a retirement community near Fort Belvoir, Virginia, on November 15, 1997, at the age of 93.

JACKLYN HAROLD LUCAS-PFC Lucas fell upon two hand grenades to save his comrades on Iwo Jima on February 20, 1945. He miraculously survived and was awarded the Medal of Honor, the youngest Marine ever to earn it, six days past his 17th birthday. Oddly enough, he was listed as a deserter at the time.

A rebellious youth, Lucas lied about his age to enlist at 14, had been in trouble several times for being AWOL, stealing beer and assaulting MP's. He deserted his supply unit in Hawaii and sneaked aboard a transport headed for the Iwo Jima invasion.

After 22 operations, he was left with only a partially disabled arm. Finishing high school and graduating from college, he was commissioned as a Lieutenant in the Army in 1961 but was discharged four years later after more bouts of drinking and fighting. Two divorces, a case where his second wife tried to hire a man to kill him, losing a business and home to IRS seizures, and arrests for trespassing, weapons and marijuana violations were some of the troubles to dog his later years. He attended the 40th anniversary of the battle of Iwo Jima on February 19, 1985, and later moved to Maryland in search of a quieter, more peaceful existence.

JACK LUMMUS-Marine First Lieutenant Lummus was posthumously awarded the Medal of Honor for destroying a series of Japanese pillboxes on Iwo Jima on March 8, 1945. Lummus was a former end for the New York Giants pro football team. At the end of his assault on the pillboxes, he stepped on a landmine, which blew both of his legs off and killed him.

DOUGLAS MacARTHUR-General MacArthur's award is unusual in a number of ways. It was the first award to the son of another Medal of Honor recipient. He was the oldest recipient at the time of his award. Presented by the Minister of Australia, it is probably the only one awarded by a foreign head of state. Additionally, he is probably one of the few men recommended for the award three times.

His first recommendation for the Medal was made by Medal-recipient General Leonard Wood following the Vera Cruz incursion in 1914. That award was denied by an awards board but not without a caustic response from the self-absorbed Captain MacArthur. He was also recommended for a Medal during World War I but that was downgraded to a Distinguished Service Cross. From his other actions and awards, especially during World War I, there can be little doubt of MacArthur's personal courage in combat. Nevertheless, like the man himself, the award he did receive is one of the most controversial since the World War II era.

In the face of the seemingly unstoppable Japanese juggernaut during the first months of the war, when it became obvious that the Philippines were lost, MacArthur and his family were evacuated to Australia. He left his second-in-command, General Jonathan Wainright, to formally surrender to the Japanese and endure three years as a POW. Wainright would be awarded his own Medal of Honor after the war. At the time, the Axis press widely lampooned MacArthur as a coward in spite of the fact that he was ordered to move to Australia.

The arrogant, imperious commander had many detractors. Some said that he politicked shamelessly for the award, some that the country was desperate for any kind of a military hero to parade before the American people in the wake of a string of defeats beginning with Pearl Harbor. Others said that it was recommended by Army Chief of Staff George Marshall as a counter to the Axis claims of cowardice. Even so, Marshall himself had to cite the award to Lindbergh for his transatlantic flight to justify MacArthur's award. Less well known but nevertheless telling is that during the same year of 1942, General Eisenhower was also nominated for the Medal of Honor but turned it down, saying the award was for combat valor and he had not done anything of that nature.

The circumstances of his award pales in comparison with most others during that conflict. MacArthur himself admitted upon his acceptance of the award that it was meant not so much for him personally as "a recognition of the indomitable courage of the gallant army which it was my honor to command."

MELVIN MAYFIELD-Army Corporal Mayfield was awarded the Medal of Honor for his actions on Luzon in the Philippine Islands on July 29, 1945. Chronologically, his was the last action of World War II that received a Medal of Honor. Following the war, he returned to farming and died on June 19, 1990, at the age of 71.

THOMAS E. McCALL-Staff Sergeant McCall of the 36th Infantry Division won a Silver Star at Salerno and received the Medal of Honor for actions at San Angelo, Italy. He left the Army after the war but later re-enlisted, served in Korea and was wounded. On September 18, 1965, McCall drowned while saving his eight-year old son from drowning.

DAVID McCAMPBELL-Commander McCampbell became the Navy's top ace with 34 kills, holding another record by shooting down 9 enemy planes in one day. On that day, June 19, 1944, McCampbell and his group of six other Navy fighters attacked 60 Japanese planes, shooting down 41 of them with no losses of their own. Besides the Medal of Honor, he received the Navy Cross, Silver Star, Legion of Merit, three Distinguished Flying Crosses and the Air Medal. He later commanded the carrier U.S.S. *Bon Homme Richard* and retired in 1964 with the rank of Captain. He was the only person to earn the nation's two highest honors (Medal of Honor and Navy Cross) on successive days. He was never shot down, never had a forced landing and never bailed out.

McCampbell remains the top-scoring Navy ace and, although

outscored by three Army Air Corps pilots, he was the top ace to survive the war. He died in 1996 at the age of 86. Four years later in July of 2000, the Navy named a new Aegis guided missile destroyer after him.

LLOYD G. McCARTER-Private McCarter of the 503rd Parachute Infantry received his Medal of Honor for several days actions in the retaking of Corregidor in the Philippines in February of 1945. Over several days, he killed over 30 enemy soldiers. McCarter committed suicide on February 2, 1956.

CHARLES L. McGAHA-Born on February 26, 1914, McGaha enlisted in the Army in October 1937. He was at Schofield Barracks, Hawaii, during the Pearl Harbor attack. He received his Medal of Honor as a Master Sergeant with the 25th Infantry Division in the Philippines on February 7, 1945. He retired from the Army as a Major in 1961. On August 8, 1984, McGaha was stabbed to death by an armed robber in his cab company in Columbus, Georgia.

THOMAS B. McGUIRE JR.-Army Air Force Major Mcguire was in an unrelenting race to overtake Richard Bong's record of 40 air victories. He ended up as the number two ace of the war with 38 victories. He crashed and was killed on January 7, 1945, while turning his airplane at low altitude with the fuel drop tanks still attached to the wings. At the time he was involved in a dogfight with Shoici Sugita, Japan's number two ace, who had 80 victories to his credit.

McGuire Air Force Base in New Jersey is named in his honor.

NICHOLAS MINUE-Army Private Minue was posthumously awarded his Medal of Honor while serving with the 1st Armored Division in Tunisia on April 28, 1943. Minue was a World War I veteran from his native land of Poland.

JOHN C. MORGAN-Army Air Corps Second Lieutenant Morgan received his Medal of Honor for heroic actions on a bombing mission over Europe on July 28, 1943. He was later shot down and became a POW on March 6, 1944. He became the only person to become a POW after receiving the Medal of Honor. After the war, he served in Korea and retired as a Colonel.

SADAO S. MUNEMORI-PFC Munemori was posthumously awarded the Medal of Honor after smothering the blast of a grenade with his body in Italy on April 5, 1945. He was the first member of the Nisei 442nd Regimental Combat Team to win the Medal and the only Japanese-American so honored during World War II.

DOUGLAS ALBERT MUNRO-Signalman First Class Munro was posthumously awarded his Medal of Honor for heroic actions while evacuating trapped Marines from Guadalcanal on September 27, 1942. He is the only U.S. Coast Guardsman to ever receive it. After accepting his Medal, his mother enlisted in the Coast Guard and served for two years.

AUDIE LEON MURPHY-Born on June 20, 1924, in rural Hunt County, Texas, diminutive (5'5 1/2", 112 pounds) Audie Murphy was rejected by both the Marine Corps and paratroopers before being accepted into the Army ten days after his 18th birthday. Landing in North Africa with the 3rd Infantry Division, he saw no combat there but made up for it following amphibious landings in Sicily, Italy and Southern France. Between March of 1944 and January of 1945, he became the most highly decorated American serviceman in World War II, surpassing Maurice Britt. In those ten months, he earned the Medal of Honor, Distinguished Service Cross, two Silver Stars, Legion of Merit, two Bronze Stars for Valor, three Purple Hearts, the French Legion of Honor, two *Croix de Guerres*, the Medal of Liberated France and the Belgian *Croix de Guerre* with Palm. With postwar awards and campaign medals, his total eventually reached 37 medals, 11 of them for valor in combat.

Surviving the war, he established a career as a movie star in Hollywood, making 44 movies, mostly low budget westerns. He was killed in a plane crash in Virginia on May 28, 1971, and was buried at Arlington National Cemetery.

ALEXANDER R. NININGER JR.-Second Lieutenant Nininger was posthumously awarded the Medal of Honor for his actions in the defense of Bataan in January of 1942. A member of the West Point Class of 1941, Nininger was the first of 37 graduates of that class to die in World War II and the only member of that class to win the nation's highest decoration.

JOSEPH TIMOTHY O'CALLAHAN-Navy Commander O'Callahan received his Medal of Honor for his actions during the attack on the carrier U.S.S. *Franklin* on March 19, 1945. The first Chaplain to win the award since the Civil War, he died on March 18, 1964.

EDWARD HENRY O'HARE-Lieutenant "Butch" O'Hare was the first Navy ace of World War II. On February 20, 1942, O'Hare shot down five enemy planes in one day and single-handedly saved the USS Lexington by his actions. After receiving the Medal of Honor for this action, he increased his score to 12. He was accidentally killed in action on November 27, 1943. Joining formation at night with a Navy TBF, the rear gunner thought he was Japanese and shot him down by mistake. Chicago's O'Hare Airport is named in his honor.

HARL PEASE JR.-Army Air Corps Captain Pease's Medal of Honor was awarded for a mission in which he was shot down near Rabaul on August 7, 1942. Although his award is posthumous, he was not killed in this action. He bailed out and was taken prisoner. On October 8, 1942, he and five other POW's were beheaded by the Japanese after being forced to dig their own graves. Pease Air Force Base in Portsmouth, New Hampshire, is named in his honor.

FRANCIS JUNIOR PIERCE-Navy Pharmacist's Mate First Class Pierce was awarded the Medal of Honor while serving as a corpsman with Marines on Iwo Jima on March 15-16, 1945.

On April 3, 1982, Pierce was serving as a Lieutenant with the Grand Rapids, Michigan, Police when he responded to a call at a high school in Rockford. An old bottle of picric acid had crystallized and chemical disposal companies refused to touch it since it had the explosive power of four sticks of dynamite. Pierce took the bottle off the shelf, put it in his pocket and took it behind the school where he dumped it in a bucket of water.

LAWSON PATERSON RAMAGE-As commanding officer of the U.S.S. *Parche*, Commander Ramage became the third Navy submariner to receive the Medal of Honor in World War II. He retired from the Navy as a Vice Admiral in 1970 and died on Easter Sunday, 1990. He was buried in Arlington National Cemetery.

THEODORE ROOSEVELT JR.-Brigadier General Roosevelt was awarded the Medal of Honor for leading troops ashore at Normandy on D-Day on June 6, 1944. Although he lived through that action, he died from a heart attack on July 13, 1944, while serving as Assistant Division Commander of the 4th Infantry Division. He was the third of former President Theodore Roosevelt's four sons to die in war.

DONALD KIRBY ROSS-Navy Machinist Ross earned his Medal of Honor on the first day of the war while serving on the battleship U.S.S. *Nevada* in Pearl Harbor. He retired from the Navy in 1956 as a Captain. On December 7, 1991, he introduced President George Bush at the ceremonies for the 50th anniversary of Pearl Harbor.

Following his death on May 27, 1992, at his request he was buried at sea in the Pacific Ocean over the resting place of the *Nevada*. The Navy named a new Aegis guided missile destroyer (DDG-71) in his honor.

WILLIAM A. SHOMO-Army Air Corps Major Shomo earned his Medal of Honor on his first combat mission on January 11, 1945. In that mission, he shot down 7 Japanese planes in one day, eclipsing the record of six in one day set by Neel Kearby a year earlier. In civilian life, he was a licensed embalmer. He retired from the Air Force in 1968 after 28 years of service and died in 1991.

DAVID MONROE SHOUP-Marine Colonel Shoup earned his Medal of Honor as the commander of all the Marines on Tarawa on November 20-22, 1943. Later rising to four-star General, he served as the Commandant of the Marine Corps from 1960-63 and died in January of 1983.

JOHN C. SJOGREN-Staff Sergeant Sjogren of the 40th Infantry

Division earned his Medal of Honor by his aggressive action in the Philippines on May 23, 1945. During this action, he destroyed 9 Japanese pillboxes and killed 43 enemy soldiers. He had been originally classified as 4-F by his draft board for "curvature of the spine" but talked his way into the service. He died on August 30, 1987, at the age of 71.

JOHN LUCIAN SMITH-Marine Major Smith earned his Medal of Honor for actions in the Solomon Islands when he shot down 16 Japanese planes in 26 days during August and September of 1942. He ended the war with a tally of 19 kills. He retired from the Marine Corps in 1961 as a full Colonel to become an aerospace executive. After being laid off work, he committed suicide on June 9, 1972.

MAYNARD H. SMITH-Born on May 19, 1911, "Snuffy" Smith was recommended for the Medal of Honor while serving as a Sergeant with the Army Air Corps on May 1, 1943. On his first combat mission, he put out a fire that saved the plane after other crewmen had bailed out. When Secretary of War Henry Stimson and a dozen generals arrived at his base to give him the Medal, he was on KP for some minor rule infraction. After the war, he went to work for the Veterans Administration and died on October 20, 1980.

JUNIOR J. SPURRIER-Born on December 14, 1922, Spurrier received his Medal of Honor while a Staff Sergeant in the 35th Infantry Division in France on November 13, 1944. His actions resulted in the deaths of 25 Germans and the capture of 4 others. After the war he became an alcoholic, refused to serve in Korea and was discharged in 1951. He served several prison terms before dying on February 25, 1984.

JAMES ELMS SWETT-Marine First Lieutenant "Zeke" Swett earned the Medal of Honor for his first air-to-air combat mission in the Solomon Islands on April 7, 1943. In this mission he became the first airman to score 7 kills in one day. William Shomo would later tie this record and David McCampbell would break it. Swett's plane was shot down by the last enemy plane he attacked that day.

Navy rescue boats had picked up a dozen downed fliers that day, both Americans and suicidal Japanese, so when they cautiously approached him in the water, a sailor yelled "Are you an American?" Swett yelled back "You're goddamn right I am!" The sailor then told his boat master that it was all right to pick the man up because he was obviously "one of them loud-mouthed Marines."

PETER TOMICH-Watertender First Class Tomich was posthumously awarded the Medal of Honor for staying at his station on the battleship U.S.S. *Utah* when she was sunk at Pearl Harbor on December 7, 1941. A native of Austria, he had no next of kin to accept the Medal for him. It was accepted by the Governor of Utah and is displayed in their state capitol.

JACK L. TREADWELL-Captain Treadwell of the 45th Infantry Division earned his Medal of Honor in Germany on March 18, 1945. Remaining in the Army, he commanded the 11th Brigade of the Americal Division in Vietnam in 1969. He retired as a full Colonel after having earned 39 medals including EVERY medal for valor in combat that the U.S. Army has available. Among his awards were the Medal of Honor, Distinguished Service Cross, Silver Star, three Legions of Merit, Distinguished Flying Cross, two Bronze Stars for Valor, Army Commendation Medal, twelve Air Medals, four Purple Hearts, two Combat Infantryman Badges and the Master Parachutist Badge. The year after his death in 1977, Treadwell had a barracks at the Army Airborne School at Fort Benning, Georgia, named in his honor.

LEON R. VANCE JR.-Army Air Corps Lieutenant Colonel Vance earned his Medal of Honor while leading a bombing mission in France on June 5, 1944. His ship was crippled by anti-aircraft fire, several crewmen killed and his right foot nearly severed. After having the rest of the crew bail out, he crash landed the ship in the ocean, refusing to leave a stranded crewman on board. A graduate of West Point in 1939, Vance survived this action but died in a crash while he was being medically evacuated to the U.S. on July 26, 1944. Vance Air Force Base in his hometown of Enid, Oklahoma, is named in his honor.

ALEXANDER ARCHER VANDEGRIFT-Major General Vandegrift earned his Medal of Honor as the commander of the 1st Marine Division on Guadalcanal, August through December of 1942. He became the first Marine in World War II to win both the Medal of Honor and the Navy Cross. He later became the first Marine four-star general and was Commandant of the Marine Corps from 1944-1947. He died on May 8, 1973, at the age of 86.

FORREST T. VOSLER-Army Air Corps Technical Sergeant Vosler earned his Medal of Honor during a bombing mission in which he served as a radioman/gunner. When the ship was crippled by gunfire and he was blinded by shrapnel, he continued to fire his guns at the enemy planes, sent distress signals before they crashed and saved another crewman from drowning. Vosler lost an eye due to his wounds and when he was discharged because of his injuries, he was quoted as saying that he "felt like a heel for leaving while his friends were still serving".

JONATHAN M. WAINRIGHT-General Wainright was the commander of all Army forces that eventually surrendered on Corregidor in the Philippines in March-May of 1942. Taken prisoner, he survived the Bataan Death March and three years in a Japanese prison camp. He was present on the U.S.S. *Missouri* when the Japanese surrendered in September of 1945. He died on September 2, 1953.

KEITH L. WARE-Ware was originally drafted in 1941. By December 26, 1944, he had risen to Lieutenant Colonel in command of the 1st Battalion, 15th Infantry, 3rd Infantry Division. On that date, he earned a Medal of Honor by wiping out a series of German machine gun nests in France. One month to the day later, he recommended another Medal of Honor for one of his men, Audie Murphy. Many years later, Ware called Murphy "the finest soldier I have ever seen in my entire military career."

Ware rose to the rank of Major General. He was killed in a helicopter crash on September 13, 1968, in Binh Long Province, South Vietnam, while serving as the commander of the 1st Infantry Division.

DAVID C. WAYBUR-First Lieutenant Waybur earned his Medal of Honor with the 3rd Infantry Division in Sicily on July 17, 1943. After receiving the Medal, he was sent to the U.S. to go on war bond tours. Although he could have finished the war that way, he requested to go back to combat duty. He was killed in action in Germany on March 28, 1945.

LOUIS HUGH WILSON JR.-Marine Captain Wilson earned his Medal of Honor on Guam on July 25-26, 1944. He later rose to four-star general and became Commandant of the Marine Corps from 1975-79, the fourth Medal of Honor recipient to hold that post.

CASSIN YOUNG-Commander Young earned his Medal of Honor on December 7, 1941, while commanding the U.S.S. *Vestal* in Pearl Harbor. Surviving that action, he was killed on November 13, 1942, on the cruiser U.S.S. *San Francisco* in the battle of Guadalcanal and Savo Island. Three other Medals of Honor were awarded to sailors on the *San Francisco* for that battle.

The navy named a destroyer (DD793) for Commander Young. Now decommissioned, it is moored next to the U.S.S. *Constitution* as a tourist attraction in Boston Harbor.

AWARDS BY SPECIAL LEGISLATION

The following awards are actually outside of the scope of this work in that they are not awards of the Medal of Honor for combat heroism but, by special acts of Congress, awards of *a* medal of honor to certain individuals for achievement and sacrifice in military service. Both Congressional acts contain the words "—the President of the United States is requested to cause a gold medal to be struck, with suitable devices, emblems and inscriptions—." These medals are not included in the Medal of Honor statistics.

COLONEL WILLIAM MITCHELL-William (Billy) Mitchell was born on December 29, 1879. Joining the Army at 18, he migrated to the Air Corps. In World War I, he was the first American pilot to fly across enemy lines. He rose to the rank of Brigadier General and became the most vocal advocate for air power. When he became too openly critical, he was court-martialed and convicted for treasonous statements. Faced with suspension, he resigned and died on February 19, 1936.

Beginning with the Pearl Harbor attack, a number of his predictions concerning air power came true and he was vindicated. On August 8, 1946, he was posthumously awarded a gold medal of honor and promoted to Major General although the medal was awarded at his permanent rank of Colonel.

THE FOUR CHAPLAINS-During the early morning hours of February 3, 1943, the U.S. Army Transport *Dorchester* was delivering another cargo of soldiers to Greenland. On its previous trip, one of the soldiers it had delivered was the future Beat novelist Jack Kerouac. But this would be its last trip.

Around 1 A.M. the ship was torpedoed by the German submarine *U-223* about 150 miles from Greenland. It would sink in less than 27 minutes. During that time, four U.S. Army Chaplains, all Lieutenants, would treat the wounded, comfort the dying, and try to keep calm and order in an impossible situation. The four Chaplains were Lt. John P. Washington, 34, a Roman Catholic priest; Lt. Clark V. Poling, 32, Dutch Reformed Church; Lt. George L. Fox, 42, Methodist; and Lt. Alexander D. Goode, 31, a Jewish Rabbi.

Two of them, Goode and Poling, were the sons of clergymen. The eldest, Lt. Fox was no stranger to either danger or courage. He had lied about his age to serve in the ambulance corps in World War I. While still a teenager, he had received the Silver Star, Purple Heart and French *Croix de Guerre* for his bravery.

Most of us can only try to imagine the wild melee that accompanies a ship full of frightened, wounded and dying men sinking in freezing waters in the middle of the night. There weren't enough life jackets or lifeboats to save everyone. Two small Coast Guard cutters were available to pick up some survivors but a third had to continue on with the convoy.

When it became obvious that all hope was lost, the four Chaplains removed their life jackets and gave them to four soldiers who had none. As the ship sank, witnesses could see the four Chaplains on the sinking deck with their arms linked and saying prayers as they sank beneath the icy, black water. Only 230 survived of the 902 aboard.

The four Chaplains were not eligible to receive the Medal of Honor because of the requirements that the heroism be performed under enemy fire. All four were awarded the Distinguished Service Cross and Purple Heart posthumously.

Years later, a Special Medal for Heroism was created and authorized by the U.S. Congress. The medals were awarded by President Eisenhower on January 18, 1961, two days before he left office.

KOREAN WAR
1950-1953

ARMY-78 awards to 78 individuals, all new recipients, 57 posthumous.

NAVY-7 awards to 7 individuals, all new recipients, 5 posthumous.

MARINE CORPS-42 awards to 42 individuals, all new recipients, 28 posthumous.

AIR FORCE-4 awards to 4 individuals, all new recipients, all 4 posthumous.

TOTAL-131 awards to 131 individuals, all new recipients, 94 posthumous.

BY RANK:

ARMY

Major General	1
Lt. Colonel	2 (2)
Captain	4 (2)
1st Lieutenant	10 (5)
2nd Lieutenant	2 (2)
Master Sergeant	6 (2)
Sergeant 1st Class	8 (8)
Sergeant	11 (7)
Corporal	16 (12)
PFC	17 (16)
Private	1 (1)

MARINES

Lt. Col.	1
Major	1
Captain	2
1st Lt.	3 (2)
2nd Lt	5 (3)
Tech. Sgt.	1
Staff Sgt	6 (4)
Sergeant	4 (4)
Corporal	6 (5)
PFC	12 (10)
Private	1

NAVY

Lieutenant j.g.	2 (1)
Hospital Corpsman	3 (3)
Hospital Corpsman 3/c	2 (1)

AIR FORCE

Major	3 (3)
Captain	1 (1)

TOTAL
ARMY   78 (57)
MARINES   42 (28)
NAV   7 (5)
AIR FORCE   4 (4)

MOST DECORATED UNITS:

ARMY

DIVISION LEVEL

2nd Infantry Div	16
25th Infantry Div	13
7th Infantry Div	12
3rd Infantry Div	11
24th Infantry Div	7
1st Cavalry Div	6

REGIMENTAL LEVEL

7th Inf., 3rd Div	8
9th Inf., 2nd Div	6
17th Inf., 7th Div	6
23rd Inf., 2nd Div	5
27th Inf., 25th Div	5

COMPANY LEVEL

Co. H, 9th Inf., 2nd Div	2
Co. F, 17th Inf., 7th Div	2
Co. C, 23rd Inf., 2nd Div	2
Co. E, 27th Inf., 25th Div	2

MARINES

REGIMENTAL LEVEL

1st Reg	10
5th Reg	10
7th Reg	21

NAVY-Awards were made to 7 Navy personnel, 2 officers and 5 enlisted men. Both officers were pilots, one in fighters and one in a helicopter. All 5 enlisted men were corpsmen serving with Marine units. One of the officers and four of the five corpsmen were posthumous awards.

AIR FORCE-These were the first awards to members of the U.S. Air Force since it became an independent military service separate from the Army in September of 1947. All four awards were posthumous to pilots. Three were flying fighter aircraft and one a B-26 bomber.

NOTE: Until the creation of a distinct Medal of Honor for the Air Force in 1960, Air Force recipients received the Army Medal of Honor.

BLACK RECIPIENTS:

Two black enlisted men in the Army were awarded Medals of Honor for service in Korea. One was a PFC and one was a Sergeant. Both were posthumous awards and both served in the 25th Infantry Division.

AGE OF RECIPIENTS:

50-59	1
40-49	1
30-39	20
20-29	92
Age 19	10

Age 18	4
Age 17	1
Unknown	2

| **AVERAGE AGE:** | 24 |

YOUNGEST RECIPIENT:

Army Corporal Charles L. Gilliland, born May 24, 1933, was a month short of his 18th birthday when he earned his Medal posthumously on April 25, 1951.

OLDEST RECIPIENT:

Major General William Frishe Dean Sr., born on August 1, 1899, was 50 when he earned his Medal on July 20-21, 1950.

NOTABLE INDIVIDUALS:

WILLIAM E. BARBER-Marine Captain Barber was a World War II veteran who had won a Silver Star and Purple Heart on Iwo Jima. He earned his Medal of Honor on November 28-December 2, 1950, in the "Frozen Chosin" Reservoir. He later retired from the Marines as a Colonel.

WILLIAM R. CHARETTE-Navy Hospital Corpsman Third Class Charette earned his Medal of Honor while serving as a medical aidman for Marines on March 27, 1953. In 1958 he was chosen to select the remains of the Unknown Soldier of World War II, traditionally done by a Medal of Honor recipient.

GEORGE ANDREW DAVIS JR.-Air Force Major Davis posthumously received his Medal of Honor for his last mission in an F-86 Saber jet fighter plane. He and his wingman attacked a dozen North Korean Migs. Davis was a World War II veteran who had previously shot down 7 Japanese fighters in the South Pacific. On his last mission, he shot down two Migs before he perished. When he died, Davis was the fourth-ranking ace in Korea with 14 victories.

THOMAS JEROME HUDNER JR.-Navy Lieutenant j.g. Hudner earned his Medal of Honor by landing his plane and trying to save a fellow flier who had been shot down. The pilot Hudner tried to save, Jessie L. Brown, was the Navy's first black aviator. Brown was posthumously awarded the Distinguished Flying Cross and a destroyer escort ship was named for him as was a street in his hometown of Hattiesburg, Mississippi.

ERNEST RICHARD KOUMA-Medals of Honor are awarded for many types of combat actions; outstanding leadership, courage under fire, rescuing wounding, saving lives and many others. But as the eminent military historian S.L.A. Marshall noted, "essentially war is the business of killing." Since its inception, many Medals of Honor have been awarded for this alone. In his Medal of Honor action in World War II, Audie Murphy was credited with killing "about 50" German soldiers and approximately 240 in all of World War II. But a soldier in the Korean War surpassed this total in a single action.

Master Sergeant Ernest Kouma, a 31-year-old tank commander in the 2nd Infantry Division, was conducting a rear guard action against a large enemy force on the night of August 31-September 1, 1951. One of his three tanks was destroyed and another withdrew, leaving his tank alone to prevent his infantry from being overrun. In a nine-hour battle, Kouma withdrew eight miles, battling the surrounding enemy with his tank's machine gun, his pistol and hand grenades. At one point he jumped out of the tank to fight them off at point-blank range. In his citation for the Medal of Honor, Kouma is credited with killing an estimated 250 enemy soldiers during this action.

CHARLES L. LORING JR.-Air Force Major Loring was a World War II veteran who had been a POW in that conflict. On November 22, 1952, he was attacking enemy gun positions in North Korea when his aircraft was hit. Rather than try to save himself, Loring dived his F-80 into the gun emplacements. He was posthumously awarded the Medal of Honor and Loring Air Force Base in Maine was named in his honor.

HIROSHI H. MIYAMURA-Born on October 6, 1925 in Gallup, New Mexico, Miyamura served with the 442nd Regimental Combat Team at the end of World War II but did not see combat with them. He was recommended for the Medal of Honor for actions on April 24-25, 1951. A Corporal in the 3rd Infantry Division, his unit was overrun in a human wave attack and he conducted a rear guard action. He was taken prisoner in this action and held for 28 months. For his safety, his Medal of Honor recommendation was classified while he was a prisoner and the Medal was awarded to him upon his release. He became the third Asia-Pacific American to earn the Medal and only the second to live to wear it.

DONN F. PORTER-Following World War II, the U.S. Army de-activated all of their elite Ranger battalions. When the Korean War began, they started reorganizing Ranger companies as a raiding and reconnaissance arm for infantry divisions. Unlike the World War II Rangers, these men were all Airborne qualified. As these companies were deactivated throughout the war and their men were transferred to regular infantry units, former Rangers became known as over-achievers. Eighteen of them from a single company earned Silver Stars serving with line units.

Sgt. Donn F. Porter, a former member of the 9th Ranger Infantry Company (Airborne), was transferred to Company G, 14th Infantry Regiment, 25th Infantry Division. On September 7, 1952, Sgt. Porter commanded a four-man outpost when attacked by two companies of enemy. Two of his men were killed almost immediately. Sgt. Porter single-handedly routed the attack, killing over 20 enemy soldiers, some of them close enough to use his bayonet, before he was killed by an artillery burst.

Sgt. Porter was posthumously awarded the Medal of Honor and buried in Arlington National Cemetery. A firing range was named for him at the Ranger Training Center at Fort Benning, Georgia. In March of 1983, apparently having no surviving relatives, his Medal of Honor was auctioned for $5,000 at Sotheby's in London.

ARCHIE VAN WINKLE-Marine Staff Sergeant Van Winkle earned his Medal of Honor near Sudong, Korea, on November 2, 1950, preventing his unit from being overrun. A Marine since he was 16 and a World War II veteran, he had been a Corporal on Guadalcanal, a Sergeant on Cape Gloucester and a Platoon Sergeant on Peleliu. He then became an aircraft gunner, winning the Distinguished Flying Cross, two Air Medals and two Purple Hearts. He retired from the Marine Corps as a Colonel in 1974.

VIETNAM WAR
1964-1973

ARMY-159 awards to 159 individuals, all new recipients, 99 posthumous.

NAVY-16 awards to 16 individuals, all new recipients, 6 posthumous.

MARINE CORPS-57 awards to 57 individuals, all new recipients, 44 posthumous.

AIR FORCE-13 awards to 13 individuals, all new recipients, 5 posthumous.

TOTAL-245 awards to 245 individuals, all new recipients, 154 posthumous.

BY RANK:

ARMY			NAVY	
Lt. Col	2	(1)	Captain	1
Major	3	(2)	Commander	1
Captain	10	(4)	Lt. Commander	1 (1)
1st Lt.	18	(12)	Lieutenant	4 (1)
2nd Lt.	5	(3)	Lieutenant jg	1
Chf.Warrant. Off.	2		Boatswains Mate 1/c	1
1st Sergeant	3	(2)	Construction Mech. 3/c	1 (1)
Sgt. 1st Class	8	(4)	Hospital Corpsman 2/c	2 (1)
Staff Sgt.	23	(13)	Hospital Corpsman 3/c	2 (1)
Sergeant	20	(15)	Engineman 1/c	1
Spec. 5/c	4	(2)	Seaman	1 (1)
Spec. 4/c	31	(19)		
Corporal	6	(6)		
PFC	23	(16)		
Private	1			

MARINES			AIR FORCE		
Captain	7	(2)	Colonel	1	(1)
1st Lieutenant	3	(1)	Lt. Colonel	1	
2nd Lieutenant	2	(2)	Major	3	
Staff Sergeant	5	(2)	Captain	5	(3)
Sergeant	5	(5)	1st Lieutenant	1	
Corporal	5	(4)	Airman 1/c	2	(1)
Lance Corporal	14	(13)			
PFC	16	(15)			

TOTALS

Army	159 (99)
Navy	16 (6)
Marines	57 (44)
Air Force	13 (5)

BY LOCATION OF ACTION:

South Vietnam	227
North Vietnam	9
Laos	6
Cambodia	2
Mediterranean Sea	1 (Vietnam era)

MOST DECORATED UNITS:

ARMY

DIVISION LEVEL:		BRIGADE/REGIMENT LEVEL:	
1st Cavalry Division	29	5th Special Forces Group	17
25th Infantry Division	21	173rd Airborne Brigade	14
101st Airborne Division	16	503rd Reg., 173rd Airbn	9
1st Infantry Division	11	7th Cav., 1st Cav. Div.	7
4th Infantry Division	11	5th Cav., 1st Cav. Div.	5
9th Infantry Division	10	12th Cav., 1st Cav. Div.	5
		27th Inf., 25th Inf. Div.	5
		506th Abn., 101st Abn. Div.	5
		8th Cav., 1st Cav. Div.	5
		8th Inf., 4th Inf. Div.	5

COMPANY LEVEL:

Co. D, 1st Bn., 12th Cavalry., 1st Cav. Div	3
Co. B, 2nd Bn., 502nd Abn., 101st Abn. Div	3
Co. A, 2nd Bn., 27th Inf., 25th Inf. Div	3

Ten companies had two Medal recipients.

BLACK RECIPIENTS:

Twenty black men were awarded the Medal of Honor for service in Vietnam. Eleven were Army enlisted men and the other two groups were unique. For the first time, Medals of Honor were awarded to black Marines (5) and black Army officers (4).

AGE OF RECIPIENTS:

40-49	11
30-39	41
20-29	169
Age 19	15
Age 18	9
AVERAGE AGE:	25

YOUNGEST RECIPIENT:

Marine Private First Class Robert Charles Burke, born November 7, 1949, was the youngest of nine 18-year-olds to earn the Medal of Honor in Vietnam. He was posthumously awarded the Medal for actions on May 17, 1968.

OLDEST RECIPIENT:

Chief Warrant Officer Michael Joseph Novosel, born September 3, 1922, was 47 when he earned the Medal on October 2, 1969. (See below)

NOTABLE INDIVIDUALS:

JAMES ANDERSON JR.-PFC Anderson posthumously earned his Medal of Honor near Cam Lo on February 28, 1967, by falling on a grenade to protect his comrades. He became the first black Marine to earn the Medal.

JOHN F. BAKER JR. and ROBERT F. FOLEY-On November 5, 1966, Company A, 2nd Battalion, 27th Infantry, 25th Infantry Division, became involved in a firefight while trying to rescue another unit engaged with the unit. In that altercation, two men in that unit would receive the Medal of Honor. They were vastly different in rank and physical size.

Captain Robert F. Foley was a West Point graduate and the commander of A Company. John F. Baker Jr. was a PFC. Foley was 6'7" tall and Baker was 5'2" tall. Both would survive their tours in Vietnam and both would remain in the Army. Baker would retire as a Master Sergeant, Foley as a Major General.

TED BELCHER-Sergeant Belcher was posthumously awarded the Medal of Honor while serving with the 25th Infantry Division on November 19, 1966. He was killed by falling on a grenade to save his men. Sergeant Belcher, 42, had also fought as an infantryman in World War II.

THOMAS W. BENNETT-Corporal Bennett was posthumously awarded the Medal of Honor while serving as a medic with the 4th Infantry Division on February 9-11, 1969. In the time-honored tradition of medical aidmen, he died while trying to save his fellow soldiers. Corporal Bennett became the second conscientious objector to win the nation's highest award and the first since World War II.

PATRICK HENRY BRADY-Major Brady, a helicopter pilot, earned his Medal of Honor on March 16-19, 1968, after making multiple flights under heavy fire to evacuate over 100 wounded men. Brady eventually advanced to the rank of Major General and became the Army Chief of Public Affairs.

PAUL WILLIAM BUCHA-Captain Bucha earned his Medal of Honor while serving with the 101st Airborne Division on March 16-19, 1968. He resigned from the Army in August of 1972 and worked for six years overseas in computers for billionaire H. Ross Perot. In 1980 Bucha started his own international marketing firm and became a multi-millionaire.

GEORGE E. DAY-Air Force Colonel Day was recommended for the Medal of Honor after he was shot down on August 26, 1967. Captured, escaping and recaptured, he earned his Medal by his actions as a POW for the next 5 1/2 years. Day had fought in World War II, Korea and Vietnam. After the war, he retired to Florida to practice law. During his military career in three wars, he had received 60 medals, 40 of them for valor in combat including the Medal of Honor, Air Force Cross, Distinguished Service Medal, two Silver Stars, Legion of Merit, Distinguished Flying Cross, three Bronze Stars, four Purple Hearts and ten Air Medals.

DAVID CHARLES DOLBY-Sergeant Dolby earned his Medal of Honor while serving with the 1st Cavalry Division on May 21, 1966. Discharged in December of 1971, he was convicted of Forgery in Hawaii in 1974.

BERNARD FRANCIS FISHER-Air Force Major Fisher earned his Medal of Honor on March 10, 1966. He landed his plane and successfully rescued a fellow airman who had crashed. Prior to 1947, the Army Air Corps was part of the Army. Even though it became a separate service that year, Air Force Medal of Honor recipients were awarded the Army Medal. Redesigned in 1960 and approved in 1965, the first newly designed Air Force Medal of Honor was presented to Major Fisher. He retired from the Air Force in 1974 as a Colonel after 27 years of service. In retirement, he farmed an 80-acre ranch near Kuna, Idaho, and (at last count) had 26 grandchildren.

JOE R. HOOPER-Sergeant Hooper earned his Medal of Honor while serving with the 101st Airborne Division on February 21, 1968. By witnesses accounts, he killed 24 men during that action. By his own account, he killed 115 men while serving in Vietnam including one he threw out of a helicopter because "he laughed at me." Commissioned as an officer in 1971, he finished the war as one of its most highly decorated men, receiving the Medal of Honor, two Silver Stars, two Bronze Stars for Valor, three Army Commendation Medals, nine Air Medals and seven Purple Hearts. He resigned from the Army as a Major in 1974 and died on May 5, 1979, at the age of 40.

CHARLES ERNEST HOSKING JR.-Master Sergeant Hosking was posthumously awarded the Medal of Honor while serving with the 5th Special Forces Group on March 21, 1967. When a Viet Cong tried to attack a group of officers with a grenade, Hosking grabbed the man and both men fatally absorbed the blast. A World War II veteran, Hosking had been wounded at the Battle of the Bulge.

ROBERT L. HOWARD-Sergeant First Class Howard received his Medal of Honor for actions on December 30, 1968, while serving with the 5th Special Forces Group. As nearly as can be determined, he is the most highly decorated American serviceman living today.

He served 54 months in Vietnam, was wounded 14 times, received the Medal of Honor, Distinguished Service Cross, 3 Silver Stars, 3 Bronze Stars, 3 Army Commendation Medals, 8 Purple Hearts and 2 Vietnamese Crosses of Gallantry among other decorations. He was recommended for the Medal of Honor three times for three separate actions in thirteen months. The first two recommendations were downgraded to lesser decorations and the last one was approved.

His father and four uncles were all paratroopers in World War II, all were wounded in combat and two died from their wounds. SFC Howard was commissioned as an officer and retired from the Army as a Colonel.

JOE M. JACKSON-Air Force Lieutenant Colonel Jackson earned his Medal of Honor for voluntarily flying his C-123 aircraft in to rescue a Combat Control Team trapped in an overrun Special Forces camp on May 12, 1968. A 27-year veteran, Jackson had flown B-

25 bombers in World War II, had flown 107 combat missions in Korea and had been one of the first Air Force pilots to fly the U-2 spy plane. He retired from the Air Force in 1971 as a full Colonel.

LAWRENCE JOEL-Specialist Sixth Class Joel earned his Medal of Honor while serving as a Combat Medic with the 173rd Airborne Brigade on November 8, 1965. In a 24-hour firefight with Viet Cong, he risked his life repeatedly to save and treat his wounded comrades. He became the first black man to receive a non-posthumous Medal of Honor since the Spanish American War. He died from natural causes on February 4, 1984.

DWIGHT H. JOHNSON-Specialist Fifth Class Johnson was awarded the Medal of Honor for aggressive actions in a firefight with a battalion of North Vietnamese on January 15, 1968, while serving with the 4th Infantry Division. On April 30, 1971, Johnson was killed while robbing a liquor store in his hometown of Detroit, Michigan.

WILLIAM A. JONES III-Air Force Colonel Jones was awarded the Medal of Honor while serving as an A-1H Skyraider pilot attempting to rescue a downed pilot on September 1, 1968. Wounded and suffering serious burns during the attempt, Jones survived the mission. On November 15, 1969, he was killed in a private plane crash in Virginia before his Medal could be awarded.

KENNETH MICHAEL KAYS-PFC Kays was awarded the Medal of Honor for his actions as a medical aidman with the 101st Airborne Division on May 7, 1970. Saving and treating numerous men under heavy fire, he lost the lower part of his left leg from his own wounds.

In August of 1979, Kays was committed to a mental institution in Illinois until he "could understand the charges against him." He was charged with Auto Theft and Possession of Marijuana.

ALAN JAY KELLOGG JR.-Marine Gunnery Sergeant Kellogg earned his Medal of Honor by being one of the few men to survive a grenade blast at close range. On March 11, 1970, an enemy grenade bounced off of his chest during a firefight. Kellogg forced the grenade down in the mud and covered it with his body.   On May 17, 1984, still serving as a Sergeant Major, Kellogg placed a wreath on the casket of the Unknown Soldier of the Vietnam War, traditionally done by a Medal of Honor recipient.

JOSEPH R. KERREY-Navy Lieutenant Junior Grade Kerrey earned his Medal of Honor while serving as a SEAL Team leader on an intelligence mission on March 14, 1969. As a result of the wounds suffered in that mission, Kerrey lost his right leg. After the war, he was elected Governor of his home state of Nebraska and, in 1989, a U.S. Senator.

ANGELO J. LITEKY-Captain Liteky earned his Medal of Honor on December 6, 1967, while serving as a Chaplain with the 199th Infantry Brigade. In heavy combat, Liteky saved over 20 wounded men, sometimes shielding them from enemy fire with his own body.

In 1975, at the age of 43, Liteky renounced the Catholic religion and married a former nun. In July of 1986, he returned his Medal of Honor in protest of President Reagan's policies in Nicaragua.

JOHN J. McGINTY III-Marine Staff Sergeant McGinty earned his Medal of Honor on July 18, 1966, when his 32-man platoon was engaged in a rear guard action against an enemy regiment. He aggressively directed a four-hour battle that killed an estimated 500 of the enemy.

McGinty had to have his left eye removed as a result of his injuries in that action. He was commissioned as an officer in August of 1967 and advanced to the rank of Captain before being medically discharged in 1976. In 1983, as a born-again Christian, he gave away all of his medals because he considered the engraving of Minerva (the Roman goddess of War) on the Medal of Honor to be blasphemous.

WILLIAM I. McGONAGLE-Navy Commander McGonagle was the recipient of the only Medal of Honor during the Vietnam era that was not for action in the Vietnam War. On June 8-9, 1967, he was commanding the intelligence ship U.S.S. *Liberty* in the Mediterranean Sea. The Six-Day War between Israel and several Arab nations had begun two days earlier. Israeli jet fighters and torpedo boats attacked his vessel, mistaking it for an Egyptian vessel. In the 75-minute attack, 34 crewmen were killed, 171 wounded and the ship badly damaged.

The commanding officer (McGonagle) was later awarded the Medal of Honor in the Washington Navy Yard instead of the traditional location of the White House, ostensibly to avoid embarrassing the Israelis. In addition, the ship's executive officer was posthumously awarded the Navy Cross. Other crewmen were awarded the Silver Star and Bronze Star medals (some posthumously), 205 received Purple Hearts (34 posthumously) and all crewmen were awarded the National Defense Service Medal, the Navy Presidential Unit Citation and the Combat Action Ribbon. This may also be the only Medal of Honor awarded for actions against a nation that was not at war with the U.S.

DAVID H. McNERNEY-First Sergeant McNerney earned his Medal of Honor by assuming command of his company of the 4th Infantry Division during heavy combat with an enemy battalion on March 22, 1967. McNerney's father had won the Distinguished Service Cross, Silver Star, two Purple Hearts and the French *Croix de Guerre* in World War I. Two of his brothers served in World War II and another brother was a Navy pilot in Vietnam. McNerney retired from the Army in 1969 after 20 years of service to become a Customs Inspector in Texas.

THOMAS R. NORRIS-Tom Norris joined the Navy intending to become a naval aviator but his eyesight wasn't up to those standards. As a second choice, he chose the SEALs, the Navy's Special Operations force.

Navy Lieutenant Norris earned his Medal of Honor while serving as a SEAL Team leader on a mission to rescue two downed pilots on April 10-13, 1972. Despite heavy opposition, his team rescued one of the pilots.

In October of 1972, before receiving his Medal of Honor, Norris was severely wounded while on an intelligence mission. He lost his left eye as a result of the wounds he suffered during that mission.

Medically discharged from the Navy, he applied to the FBI. After receiving a medical waiver from Director William Webster and passing all the other tests required of agent applicants, he completed a 20-year career as an FBI agent. (See Michael Edwin Thornton).

MICHAEL J. NOVOSEL-Novosel joined the Army Air Corps in 1941 at the age of 19. He flew combat missions over Japan in B-29's and flew one of the B-29's over the surrender ceremonies in Tokyo Bay in September of 1945. Five feet, four inches tall, he became a Lieutenant Colonel in the Air Force Reserve and a commercial airline pilot after the war.

When the Air Force refused to recall him for combat duty in Vietnam at the age of 42, he resigned his commission and enlisted in the Army as a Warrant Officer flying helicopters.

He earned his Medal of Honor flying a medical evacuation helicopter on October 2, 1969, at the age of 47. He and his son were the only father-son medical evacuation team in Vietnam. Between them, they evacuated over 8,000 casualties during the war. Novosel retired on March 1, 1985, as the last World War II aviator on active duty.

RICHARD A. PENRY-Sergeant Penry earned his Medal of Honor while serving on a night ambush mission with the 199th Infantry Brigade on January 31, 1970. During that mission, he saved 18 men.

In 1973, Penry was arrested in California for Distribution of Cocaine.

WILLIAM THOMAS PERKINS JR.-Marine Corporal Perkins was posthumously awarded the Medal of Honor for falling on a grenade during combat with several enemy companies on October 12, 1967. Perkins is the only Combat Photographer to win the decoration.

RILEY L. PITTS-Captain Pitts was posthumously awarded a Medal of Honor after his actions on October 31, 1967, with the 25th Infantry Division. In combat with a large enemy force, Pitts threw himself on a grenade, which failed to explode. He was later mortally wounded in the same action. Pitts was buried in Oklahoma City, Oklahoma, where he has a park named for him.

STEPHEN W. PLESS-Marine Major Pless earned the Medal of Honor while serving as a helicopter gunship pilot on August 19, 1967. Aggressively attacking an enemy force overrunning an American unit, he then loaded his helicopter with wounded men. When he flew out of the area, the helicopter was so overloaded that it settled into the ocean four times before becoming airborne.

Major Pless was killed in a motorcycle accident in Pensacola, Florida, on July 20, 1969.

WILLIAM D. PORT-Sergeant Port was awarded a posthumous Medal of Honor while serving with the 1st Cavalry Division on January 12, 1968. During combat, he threw himself on an enemy grenade to shield his comrades. Port was not killed in this action but was taken prisoner. He remained a POW for ten months before dying on November 27, 1968. In August of 1985, his remains were recovered and were buried in Arlington National Cemetery.

CHARLES CALVIN ROGERS-Lieutenant Colonel Rogers earned his Medal of Honor on November 1, 1968, while serving as a battalion commander with the 1st Infantry Division defending a fire support base from overwhelming enemy opposition.

Rogers has college degrees in Mathematics and Chemistry. He was promoted to Major General in 1980. He is the highest ranking black man to ever receive the Medal of Honor.

RUPPERT L. SARGENT-First Lieutenant Sargent was posthumously awarded the Medal of Honor while serving with the 25th Infantry Division on March 15, 1967. While clearing tunnels of Viet Cong, Sargent threw himself on two grenades to protect his men and was killed by the explosions.

He became the first black officer to receive the Medal of Honor. His widow, a Jehovah's Witness, refused to accept the Medal until it was agreed the presentation would be made in private with no public ceremony.

MARVIN G. SHIELDS-The U.S. Navy's Seabees (Construction Battalions-C.B.'s) made an enviable reputation during World War

II mostly by turning island jungles into airplane landing strips in the Pacific Theater. Their fame soared when John Wayne starred in the movie *The Fighting Seabees* in 1944.

Construction Mechanic Third Class Marvin G. Shields was assigned to help construct the defenses of the Army Special Forces camp at Dong Xoai on June 10, 1965, when the camp was attacked by a Viet Cong regiment. Mortally wounded while participating in the combat, Shields was posthumously awarded the Medal of Honor for his actions. This is the same battle in which Army Special Forces Lieutenant Charles Q. Williams also received the Medal of Honor. Shields is the only Navy Seabee to be so honored.

JAMES B. STOCKDALE-Navy Captain Stockdale was shot down as a Navy fighter pilot on September 4, 1965. He became and remained the highest ranking American POW in the war. Steadfastly resistant to his captor's torture and brainwashing techniques, he spent four years in solitary confinement. He was released on February 12, 1973, after 2,714 days of confinement. He was awarded the Medal of Honor for his actions as a POW. In 1992, he ran for Vice-President of the United States with H. Ross Perot. Incidentally, his middle name is Bond.

MICHAEL EDWIN THORNTON-Navy Petty Officer Thornton was awarded the last Medal of Honor of the Vietnam War while serving as a member of a SEAL Team on an intelligence mission on October 31, 1972. During that mission, the officer in charge of the team was severely wounded. Thornton went back and rescued the officer, saving his life. The officer he rescued was Lieutenant Thomas Norris, also a Medal of Honor recipient.

Thornton served four tours in Vietnam and retired from the Navy as a Lieutenant.

CHARLES JOSEPH WATTERS-Major Watters was posthumously awarded the Medal of Honor while serving as a Chaplain with the 173rd Airborne Brigade on November 19, 1967. Unarmed, he was mortally wounded while rescuing and aiding wounded men. He was killed by an American 500-pound bomb that missed its target.

Watters' uncle had been John J. Doran who received the Navy Medal of Honor in 1898.

CHARLES Q. WILLIAMS-First Lieutenant Williams earned his Medal of Honor while serving with the 5th Special Forces Group on June 9-10, 1965. His heroic actions occurred when an overwhelming force of Viet Cong attempted to overrun the Special Forces camp at Dong Xoai. Williams retired as a Major. He died in Columbia, South Carolina, on October 15, 1982, at the age of 49. He died from cancer, which was allegedly induced by his exposure to Agent Orange during the war.

JAMES E. WILLIAMS-Navy Boatswains Mate First Class Williams earned his Medal of Honor while serving on a River Patrol Boat (PBR) on October 31, 1966. He and his crew engaged in a three-hour machinegun battle with a fleet of more than 65 enemy sampans.

Born in 1930, he was a veteran of both Korea and Vietnam. Williams is probably the most highly decorated enlisted man in U.S. Navy history. Besides the Medal of Honor, he earned the Navy Cross, two Silver Stars, the Legion of Merit for Valor, two Navy and Marine Corps Medals for non-combat heroism, three Bronze Stars for Valor, two Navy Commendation Medals for Valor, three Purple Hearts and fourteen other campaign and service medals. When Williams retired from the Navy he became a Deputy United States Marshal.

SOMALIA
1993

ARMY- 2 awards to 2 individuals, both new recipients, both posthumous.

These two awards were made to two U.S. Army Special Forces sergeants who were members of a Delta Force sniper team with Task Force Ranger battling Somalian rebels in Mogadishu on October 3, 1993. They volunteered to attempt the rescue of a helicopter crew that had been shot down. Both awards were posthumous. This battle is the subject of the movie *Black Hawk Down*.

BY RANK:

Master Sergeant	1 (1)
Sergeant First Class	1 (1)

AGE OF RECIPIENTS:

30-39	2

AVERAGE AGE: 34

YOUNGEST RECIPIENT:

Army Master Sergeant Gary Ivan Gordon, born August 30, 1960, was 33 when he earned his Medal posthumously on October 3, 1993.

OLDEST RECIPIENT:

Army Sergeant First Class Randall David Shughart, born August 13, 1958, was 35 when he earned his Medal posthumously on October 3, 1993.

NOTABLE INDIVIDUALS:

GARY IVAN GORDON and RANDALL DAVID SHUGHART- Task Force Ranger consisted of elements of an Army Ranger battalion and Delta Force, the Army's top secret anti-terrorism unit. Both Sergeants Gordon and Shughart were members of Delta Force.

The Somalia operation was a peacekeeping and famine relief effort that was attempted in the midst of a vicious civil war. In the resulting battle of October 3, 1993, four helicopters were shot down, 18 soldiers died and 73 were wounded. The entire helicopter crew that Gordon and Shughart were trying to rescue were killed except for the pilot, Michael Durant. Durant was captured and released after eleven days. President Clinton immediately halted the Somalia operation, much to the dissatisfaction of many of the members of the mission.

At the Medal of Honor presentation ceremony in the White House on May 23, 1994, Randy Shughart's father refused to shake hands with President Clinton and told him he "wasn't fit to be the commander-in-chief."

APPENDICES

THE MELTING POT II

O f the 3,440 persons who have been awarded Medals of Honor, 746 of them were born in 38 other countries, more than one-fifth of the total. Predictably, most of them have come from the Anglo-Saxon roots that most of America considered their "mother countries". The British Isles, Ireland and Canada provided 461 or 62 percent of the foreign born Medal of Honor recipients. The foreign born came from the following countries:

Ireland	258
Germany	128
England	99
Canada	57
Scotland	39
Norway	20
France	18
Sweden	16
Prussia	10
Austria	9
Denmark	9
Wales	8
Holland	7
West Indies	7
Switzerland	6
Philippines	6
Mexico	5
Russia	5
Finland	4
Italy	4
Puerto Rico	4
Australia	3
Malta	3
Belgium	3
China	2
Hungary	2
India	2
Spain	2

Bermuda	1
Chile	1
Cuba	1
Europe	1
Greece	1
Montenegro	1
Poland	1
Sandwich Islands	1
Serbia	1
Yugoslavia	1

They served in every post-Civil War conflict America had except for the campaigns in Haiti, Nicaragua, the Dominican Republic and the 1911 actions in the Philippines where the small numbers of Medals awarded precluded them. They served America in the following services:

U.S. Army	459
U.S. Navy	254
U.S. Marine Corps	32
U.S. Coast Guard	1

Like most groups, they followed patterns but were also unpredictable. For instance, it could be predicted that citizens of the seafaring nations or islands would gravitate to the Navy. As a result, 15 of the 20 Norwegians were sailors as were 6 of the 9 Danes, 10 of the 16 Swedes, 3 of the 4 Finns, 5 of the 7 West Indians, both the Spaniards and the Cuban, Chilean, Bermudan and Sandwich Islander. Likewise only 1 of the 10 Prussians was a sailor nor were the Montenegrin, Pole, Mexicans, Hungarians, Italians, Swiss or Greek. Conversely however, 4 of the 9 landlocked Austrians were sailors as were 2 of the Philippine Islanders.

BLACK RECIPIENTS:

Civil War	25	18 Army	7 Navy
Indian Campaigns	18	18 Army	
Interim 1871-1901	7		7 Navy (8 awards- one double award)
Spanish-American War	7	6 Army	1 Navy
World War I	1	1 Army	
World War II	7	7 Army	
Korea	2	2 Army	
Vietnam	20	15 Army	5 Marine Corps

TOTAL   **88 awards to 87 men**

67 Army   **15 Navy**   **5 Marine Corps**

RANK-NAME-SERVICE-DATE OF ACTION OR AWARD

Sergeant William H. Carney, USA, July 18, 1863.
Contraband Robert Blake, USN, December 25, 1863.
Seaman Joachim Pease, USN, June 19, 1864.
Private William H. Barnes, USA, July 12, 1864.
Sergeant Decatur Dorsey, USA, July 30, 1864.
Landsman William H. Brown, USN, August 5, 1864.
Landsman Wilson Brown, USN, August 5, 1864.
Landsman John Lawson, USN, August 5, 1864.
Engineer's Cook James Mifflin, USN, August 5, 1864.
First Sergeant Powhatan Beatty, USA, September 29, 1864.
First Sergeant James H. Bronson, USA, September 29, 1864.
Sergeant Major Christian A. Fleetwood, USA, September 29, 1864.
Private James Gardiner, USA, September 29, 1864.
Sergeant James H. Harris, USA, September 29, 1864.
Sergeant Major Thomas R. Hawkins, USA, September 29, 1864.
Sergeant Alfred B. Hinton, USA, September 29, 1864.
Sergeant Major Milton M. Holland, USA, September 29, 1864.
First Sergeant Alexander Kelly, USA, September 29, 1864.
First Sergeant Robert Pinn, USA, September 29, 1864.
First Sergeant Edward Ratcliff, USA, September 29, 1864.
Private Charles Veal, USA, September 29, 1864.

Corporal Miles James, USA, September 30, 1864.
Corporal Andrew Jackson Smith, USA, November 30, 1864.
Private Bruce Anderson, USA, January 15, 1865.
Landsman Aaron Sanderson, USN, March 17, 1865.
Sergeant Emanuel Stance, USA, May 20, 1870
Seaman Joseph B. Noil, USN, December 26, 1872.
Private Adam Paine, USA, September 26-27, 1874.
*Private Pompey Factor, USA, April 25, 1875.
*Trumpeter Isaac Payne, USA, April 25, 1875.
*Sergeant John Ward, USA, April 25, 1875.
Corporal Clinton Greaves, USA, January 24, 1877.
Sergeant Thomas Boyne, USA, May 29, 1879.
Sergeant John Denny, USA, September 18, 1879.
Sergeant Henry Johnson, USA, October 2-5, 1879.
Cooper William Johnson, USN, November 14, 1879.
Sergeant George Jordan, USA, May 14, 1880.
Seaman John Smith, USN, September 19, 1880.
Ordinary Seaman John Davis, USN, February 1881.
Sergeant Thomas Shaw, USA, August 12, 1881.
Private Augustus Walley, USA, August 16, 1881.
First Sergeant Moses Williams, USA, August 16, 1881.
Sergeant Brent Woods, USA, August 19, 1881.
Ordinary Seaman Robert Sweeney, USN, Oct.26,1881, &
Dec.20, 1883.
Sergeant Benjamin Brown, USA, May 11, 1889.
Corporal Isaiah Mays, USA, May 11, 1889.
Sergeant William McBryar, USA, March 7, 1890.
Corporal William O. Wilson, USA, September 17, 1891.
Ship's Cook Daniel Atkins, USN, February 11, 1898.
Private Dennis Bell, USA, June 30, 1898.
Private Fitz Lee, USA, June 30, 1898.
Private William H. Thompkins, USA, June 30, 1898.
Private George H. Wanton, USA, June 30, 1898.
Sergeant Major Edward L. Baker Jr., USA, July 1, 1898.
Private Charles P. Cantrell, USA, July 1, 1898.
Fireman First Class Robert Penn, USN, July 20, 1898.
Seaman Alphonse Girandy, USN, March 31, 1901.
Corporal Freddie Stowers, USA, September 28, 1918.

Private George Watson, USA, March 8, 1943.
Staff Sergeant Ruben Rivers, USA, November 15-19, 1944.
Captain Charles L. Thomas, USA, December 14, 1944.
First Lieutenant John R. Fox, USA, December 26, 1944.
Staff Sergeant Edward A. Carter Jr., USA, March 23, 1945.
First Lieutenant Vernon J. Baker, USA, April 5-6, 1945.
PFC Willy F. James Jr., USA, April 7, 1945.
PFC William Thompson, USA, August 6, 1950.
Sergeant Cornelius H. Charlton, USA, June 2, 1951.
PFC Milton L. Olive III, USA, October 22, 1965.
Specialist Sixth Class Lawrence Joel, USA, November 8, 1965.
Sergeant Donald Russell Long, USA, June 30, 1966.
PFC James Anderson Jr., USMC, February 28, 1967.
Platoon Sergeant Matthew Leonard, USA, February 28, 1967.
First Lieutenant Ruppert L. Sargent, USA, March 15, 1967.
Sergeant Rodney Maxwell Davis, USMC, September 6, 1967.
Sergeant First Class Webster Anderson, USA, October 15, 1967.
Captain Riley L. Pitts, USA, October 31, 1967.
Specialist Fifth Class Clarence E. Sasser, USA, January 10, 1968.
Specialist Fifth Class Dwight H. Johnson, USA, January 15, 1968.
Sergeant First Class Eugene Ashley Jr., USA, February 6-7, 1968.
Staff Sergeant Clifford Chester Sims, USA, February 21, 1968.
PFC Ralph H. Johnson, USMC, March 5, 1968.
Lieutenant Colonel Charles Calvin Rogers, USA, November 1, 1968.
First Lieutenant John E. Warren Jr., USA, January 14, 1969.
PFC Garfield M. Langhorn, USA, January 15, 1969.
PFC Oscar P. Austin, USMC, February 23, 1969.
PFC Robert H. Jenkins Jr., USMC, March 5, 1969.
Sergeant First Class William Maud Bryant, USA, March 24, 1969.

*These three men were freedmen of mixed Seminole and Negro heritage. Therefore they are listed under both Black Recipients and American Indian recipients.

Hispanic Recipients:

Civil War	3
Boxer Rebellion	1
World War I	1
World War II	13
Korea	9
Vietnam	15
TOTAL	42

RANK-NAME-SERVICE-DATE OF ACTION OR AWARD

Corporal Joseph H. Decastro, USA, July 3, 1863
Seaman John Ortega, USN, December 31, 1864.
Ordinary Seaman Phillip Bazaar, USN, January 15, 1865.
Private France Silva, USMC, June 28/August 17, 1900
.Private David B. Barkley, USA, November 9, 1918
.Private Joe P. Martinez, USA, May 26, 1943.
Staff Sergeant Lucien Adams, USA, October 28, 1944.
Staff Sergeant Marcario Garcia, USA, November 27, 1944.
Sergeant Jose M. Lopez, USA, December 17, 1944.
Master Sergeant Nicholas Oresko, USA, January 23, 1945.
PFC Jose F. Valdez, USA, January 25, 1945.
Technical Sergeant Cleto Rodriguez, USA, February 9, 1945.
PFC Manuel Perez Jr., USA, February 13, 1945.
PFC Silvestre S. Herrera, USA, March 15, 1945.
Staff Sergeant Ysmael R. Villegas, USA, March 20, 1945.
PFC Harold Gonsalves, USMC, April 15, 1945.
PFC David M. Gonzales, USA, April 25, 1945.
PFC Alejandro R. Renteria Ruiz, USA, April 28, 1945.
First Lieutenant Baldomero Lopez, USMC, September 15, 1950.
PFC Eugene Arnold Obregon, USMC, September 26, 1950.
Sergeant Joseph C. Rodriguez, USA, May 21, 1951.
Corporal Rodolfo P. Hernandez, USA, May 31, 1951.
PFC Edward Gomez, USMC, September 14, 1951.
PFC Fernando Luis Garcia, USMC, September 5, 1952.
Corporal Benito Martinez, USA, September 6, 1952.

Staff Sergeant Ambrosio Guillen, USMC, July 25, 1953.
Master Sergeant Ola L. Mize, USA, June 10/11, 1953.
Specialist Fourth Class Daniel Fernandez, USA, February 18, 1966.
Specialist Fourth Class Albert Rascon, USA, March 16, 1966
Captain Euripides Rubio, USA, November 8, 1966.
First Sergeant Maximo Yabes, USA, February 26, 1967.
PFC Carlos James Lozada, USA, November 20, 1967.
Sergeant Alfredo Gonzalez, USMC, February 4, 1968.
Major M. Sando Vargas Jr., USMC, April 30/May 2, 1968.
Master Sergeant Roy P. Benavidez, USA, May 2, 1968.
Specialist Hector Santiago-Colon, USA, June 28, 1968.
Lance Corporal Jose Francisco Jimenez, USMC, August 28, 1969.
PFC Ralph E. Dias, USMC, November 12, 1969.
Specialist Fourth Class John P. Baca, USA, February 10, 1970.
Lance Corporal Emilio A. De La Garza, USMC, April 11, 1970.
Lance Corporal Miguel Keith, USMC, May 8, 1970.
Warrant Officer Louis R. Rocco, USA, May 24, 1970.

Asia-Pacific American Recipients:

Phillipines, 1911	1
World War II	24
Korea	3
Vietnam	3
TOTAL	**31**

RANK-NAME-SERVICE-DATE OF ACTION OR AWARD

Private Jose B. Nisperos, USA, September 24, 1911.
Sergeant Jose Calugas, USA, January 16, 1942.
Private Mikio Hasemoto, USA, November 29, 1943.
Private Shizuya Hayashi, USA, November 29, 1943.
Sergeant Allan M. Ohata, USA, November 29-30, 1943.
Staff Sergeant Rudolph B. Davila, USA, May 28, 1944.
Technical Sergeant Yeiki Kobashigawa, USA, June 2, 1944.
Private Shinyei Nakamine, USA, June 2, 1944.
PFC Kiyoshi K. Muranaga, USA, June 26, 1944.
PFC William K. Nakamura, USA, July 4, 1944.
PFC Frank H. Ono, USA, July 4, 1944.
PFC Kaoru Moto, USA, July 7, 1944.
Technical Sergeant Ted T. Tanouye, USA, July 7, 1944.
Staff Sergeant Kazuo Otani, USA, July 15, 1944.
Private Masato Nakae, USA, August 19, 1944.
Private Barney F. Hajiro, USA, October 19-29, 1944.
Staff Sergeant Robert T. Kuroda, USA, October 20, 1944.
Captain Francis B. Wai, USA, October 20, 1944.
Technician Fifth Grade James K. Okubo, USA, October 28-29, 1944.
Private George T. Sakato, USA, October 29, 1944.
PFC Joe M. Nishimoto, USA, November 7, 1944.
PFC Sadao S. Munemori, USA, April 5, 1945Technical
Sergeant Yukio Okutsu, USA, April 7, 1945.
Private Joe Hayashi, USA, April 20-22, 1945.
Second Lieutenant Daniel K. Inouye, USA, April 21, 1945.
Corporal Hiroshi H. Miyamura, USA, April 24-25, 1951.

Sergeant Leroy A. Mendonca, USA, July 4, 1951.
PFC Herbert K. Pililaau, USA, September 17, 1951.
Staff Sergeant Elmelindo Rodriques Smith, USA, February 16, 1967.
First Sergeant Rodney James Tadashi Yano, USA, January 1, 1969.
Corporal Terry Terno Kawamura, USA, March 20, 1969.

RECIPIENTS OF AMERICAN INDIAN DESCENT:

Indian Campaigns	15
World War II	5
Korea	2
TOTAL	22

RANK-NAME-SERVICE-DATE OF ACTION OR AWARD

Sergeant Co-Rux-Te-Chod-Ish, USA, July 8, 1869.
Sergeant Alchesay, USA, April 12, 1875.
Sergeant Blanquet, USA, April 12, 1875.
Indian Scout Chiquito, USA, April 12, 1875.
Corporal Elsatsoosu, USA, April 12, 1875.
Sergeant Jim, USA, April 12, 1875.
Indian Scout Kelsay, USA, April 12, 1875.
Indian Scout Kosoha, USA, April 12, 1875.
Private Machol, USA, April 12, 1875.
Indian Scout Nannasaddie, USA, April 12, 1875
.Indian Scout Nantaje (Nantahe), USA, April 12, 1875
.Private Pompey Factor, USA, April 25, 1875.
Trumpeter Isaac Payne, USA, April 25, 1875.
Sergeant John Ward, USA, April 25, 1875.
Sergeant Rowdy, USA, March 7, 1890.
Second Lieutenant Ernest Childers, USA, September 22, 1943.
First Lieutenant Jack C. Montgomery, USA, February 22, 1944.
Technical Sergeant Van Thomas Barfoot, USA, May 23, 1944.
Commander Ernest Edwin Evans, USN, October 25, 1944.
PFC John N. Reese Jr., USA, February 9, 1945.
Corporal Mitchell Red Cloud Jr., USA, November 5, 1950.
PFC Charles George, USA, November 30, 1952.

Jewish Recipients:

Civil War	6
Indian Campaigns	2
Haiti	1
World War I	3
World War II	3
Vietnam	2
TOTAL	17

RANK-NAME-SERVICE-DATE OF ACTION OR AWARD

Private Benjamin Levy, USA, June 30, 1862.
Private David Orbansky, USA, 1862/1863.
Sergeant Henry Heller, USA, May 2, 1863.
Sergeant Major Abraham Cohn, USA, May 8, 1864.
Sergeant Leopold Karpeles, USA, May 8, 1864.
Corporal Isaac Gause, USA, September 13, 1864.
Private Charles Gardner (Simon Suhler), USA, Aug./Oct., 1868.
Sergeant George Geiger, USA, June 25, 1876.
Private Samuel Gross (Marguiles), USMC, November 17, 1915.
First Sergeant Sydney G. Gumpertz, USA, September 29, 1918.
First Sergeant Benjamin Kaufman, USA, October 4, 1918.
Sergeant William Sawelson, USA, October 26, 1918.
Captain Benjamin L. Salomon, USA, July 7, 1944.
Second Lieutenant Raymond Zussman, USA, September 12, 1944.
Staff Sergeant Isadore S. Jachman, USA, January 4, 1945.
Captain Jack H. Jacobs, USA, March 9, 1968.
Sergeant John L. Levitow, USAF, February 24, 1969.

NOTE: While the above lists for Black, Hispanic and Jewish Medal of Honor recipients are believed to be complete and accurate, there are almost certainly other recipients of those descents whose heritage is not known at this time.

ACCREDITATION

Medal of Honor recipients are usually accredited to specific states in one of two ways. One way is by the recipient's state of birth and the other is by the state in which they entered military service. In many cases of foreign-born recipients, especially during the Civil War when most units were state-raised militias, the Medal was accredited to the parent state of the recipient's unit. Records of the past being what they are, in some cases neither the recipient's place of birth nor where he entered service is recorded and thus some Medals are not accredited to any state. Conversely, some Medals are accredited to both the state of birth and the state of enlistment or induction. For these reasons, the totals are not precise.

The following list shows, by each state:

1. How many Medal of Honor recipients were born in each state.

2. How many recipients are accredited to each state as the state of their original enlistment into military service. When a recipient was both born in and originally enlisted in the same state, he is counted under both columns.

STATE	BY BIRTH	BY ENLISTMENT
Alabama	25	21
Alaska	1	0
Arizona	15	15
Arkansas	21	11
California	51	129
Colorado	12	23
Connecticut	58	56
Delaware	13	13
District of Columbia	31	39
Florida	13	20
Georgia	25	21
Hawaii	24	20
Idaho	12	9
Illinois	106	205
Indiana	67	74

Iowa	31	53
Kansas	21	28
Kentucky	53	42
Louisiana	20	22
Maine	81	66
Maryland	67	49
Massachusetts	169	263
Michigan	72	107
Minnesota	25	46
Mississippi	13	17
Missouri	47	77
Montana	3	8
Nebraska	20	20
Nevada	0	2
New Hampshire	47	36
New Jersey	69	93
New Mexico	10	8
New York	463	661
North Carolina	29	19
North Dakota	5	17
Ohio	216	252
Oklahoma	22	20
Oregon	6	13
Pennsylvania	330	376
Rhode Island	25	30
South Carolina	30	29
South Dakota	4	5
Tennessee	38	26
Texas	56	70
Utah	4	5
Vermont	43	47
Virginia	62	50
Washington	19	33
West Virginia	44	45
Wisconsin	43	49
Wyoming	2	3

Total Number Of Medals Awarded:

ARMY

2405 Army Medals of Honor have been awarded:
2,338 awards to 2,334 individual soldiers (4 received double awards)
4 awards to Army Air Service members in World War I
38 awards to Army Air Corps and Army Air Force members in World War II
4 awards to Air Force members in Korea
6 awards to Marines (5 double awards of the Army and Navy Medal, 1 award of the Army Medal only, all in World War I)
6 awards to civilians (5 men and 1 woman)
9 Unknown Soldiers (posthumously)
424 awards were posthumous

NAVY, MARINE CORPS AND COAST GUARD

1041 Navy Medals of Honor have been awarded:
743 awards to 735 individual sailors (8 received double awards)
295 awards to 293 individual Marines (2 were double recipients of the Navy Medal only)
1 Coast Guardsman (posthumously)
2 civilians serving with the Navy
52 Navy awards have been posthumous
128 Marine awards have been posthumous

AIR FORCE

13 Air Force Medals of Honor have been awarded to:
13 airmen
5 awards were posthumous

TOTAL-3,459 Medals awarded to 3,440 individuals.

ALL INDIVIDUALS BY SERVICE AND COMMISSIONED STATUS:

	Officers	Enlisted	Total
U.S. Army	600	1,776	2,376
U.S. Navy	95	640	735
U.S. Marine Corps	71	223	294
U.S. Air Force	15	2	17
U.S. Coast Guard	0	1	1
Unknown Soldiers	????	????	9
Civilians	0	0	8
TOTALS	781	2,642	3,440

NOTE: By virtue of their usual level of education, Surgeons, Assistant Surgeons and Chaplains are considered to be officers whether formally commissioned as such or not for the purposes of the statistics in this table.

ALL AWARDS/ALL WARS BY RANK:

U.S. ARMY

GENERAL	2	
LT. GENERAL	0	
MAJOR GENERAL	5	
BRIG. GENERAL	13	(3)
COLONEL	41	(2)
LT. COLONEL	36	(10)
MAJOR	51	(9)
CAPTAIN	144	(19)
1st LT.	194	(35)
2nd LT.	86	(27)
LIEUTENANT (grade unk.)	9	
FLIGHT OFFICER	1	
CHIEF WARRANT OFFICER	2	
SURGEON	4	
ASSISTANT SURGEON	8	
SERGEANT MAJOR	21	(1)
FIRST SERGEANT	95	(7)
MASTER SERGEANT	10	(3)
SERGEANT FIRST CLASS	17	(13)
STAFF SERGEANT	64	(34)
TECHNICAL SERGEANT	24	(6)
COMMISSARY SERGEANT	5	
QUARTERMASTER SERGEANT	4	
COLOR SERGEANT	3	(1)
SERGEANT	398	(60)
TECHNICIAN 5TH GRADE	6	(5)
TECHNICIAN 4TH GRADE	2	(2)
SPECIALIST 5TH CLASS	4	(2)
SPECIALIST 4TH CLASS	31	(19)
CORPORAL	267	(33)
PRIVATE FIRST CLASS	111	(76)
PRIVATE	651	(48)

PRINCIPAL MUSICIAN	1
MUSICIAN	17
CHIEF BUGLER	4
BUGLER	6
TRUMPETER	4
DRUMMER	3
SADDLER	4
WAGONER	2
FARRIER	7
BLACKSMITH	8
INDIAN SCOUT	6
HOSPITAL STEWARD	1
CHAPLAIN	3
ARTIFICER	2
CIVILIAN SURGEON	1 (Civilian Contract Acting Assistant Surgeon)
CIVILIAN SCOUT	3
CIVILIAN GUIDE	2
UNKNOWN SOLDIERS	9 (9)
TOTAL	**2392* (424)**

*One Army double recipient, Frank Baldwin, was awarded one Medal during the Civil War at the rank of Captain and another in the Indian Campaigns at the rank of 1st Lieutenant and is included under both ranks.

U.S. NAVY

REAR ADMIRAL	4 (3)
CAPTAIN	8 (4)
COMMANDER	19 (4)
LT. COMMANDER	11 (3)
LIEUTENANT	28 (4)
LIEUTENANT j.g.	10 (3)
ENSIGN	13 (4)

APPRENTICE	3	
APPRENTICE 1/c	3	
ARMORER	1	
AVIATION CHIEF ORD. MAN	1	
BLACKSMITH	2	
BOATSWAINS MATE	37	
BOATSWAINS MATE 1/c	10	(2)
BOATSWAINS MATE 2/C	7	(1)
BOILERMAKER	2	
BOY 2/C	2	
BOY 3/C	1	
CABIN BOY	1	
CAPT. OF THE AFTERGUARD	7	
CAPT. OF THE FORECASTLE	16	
CAPTAIN OF THE FORETOP	2	
CAPTAIN OF THE HOLD	3	
CAPTAIN OF THE MAINTOP	2	
CAPT. OF THE MIZZENTOP	1	
CAPTAIN OF THE TOP	14	
2nd CAPTAIN OF THE TOP	1	
CARPENTER	1	
CARPENTERS MATE	2	
CARPENTERS MATE 2/C	1	
CARPENTERS MATE 3/C	2	
CHIEF BOATSWAIN	3	(1)
CHIEF BOATSWAINS MATE	9	
CHIEF CARPENTERS MATE	4	
CHIEF ELECTRICIAN	1	
CHIEF GUNNER	2	
CHIEF GUNNERS MATE	7	
CHIEF MACHINIST	4	
CHIEF MACHINISTS MATE	5	(1)
CHIEF MASTER AT ARMS	2	
CHIEF METALSMITH	1	
CHIEF QUARTERGUNNER	1	
CHIEF QUARTERMASTER	4	
CHIEF WATERTENDER	7	(2)
CONSTRUCTION MECHANIC 3/C	1	(1)

COAL HEAVER	10	
COAL PASSER	1	
CONTRABAND	1	
COOPER	1	
COPPERSMITH	1	
COXSWAIN	56	
ELECTRICIAN 3/C	1	
ENGINEMAN 1/c	1	
FIREMAN	4	
FIREMAN 1/C	17	
FIREMAN 2/C	8	
GUNNER	1	
GUNNERS MATE	6	
GUNNERS MATE 1/C	8	(1)
GUNNERS MATE 2/C	3	
GUNNERS MATE 3/C	4	
HOSPITAL APPRENTICE	2	
HOSPITAL APPRENTICE 1/C	4	(1)
HOSPITAL CORPSMAN	3	(3)
HOSPITAL CORPSMAN 2/C	2	(1)
HOSPITAL CORPSMAN 3/C	4	(2)
HOSPITAL STEWARD	1	
LANDSMAN	51	(1)
WARRANT MACHINIST	1	
MACHINIST	2	
MACHINIST 1/C	3	
MACHINISTS MATE	1	
MACHINISTS MATE 1/C	3	(1)
MACHINISTS MATE 2/C	1	
MASTER AT ARMS	4	
MATE	1	
OILER	2	
ORDINARY SEAMAN	49	
ORD SEAMAN APPRNTCE	1	
PAYMASTERS STEWARD	2	
PHARMACISTS MATE 1/C	3	(1)
PHARMACISTS MATE 2/C	2	(1)
PHARMACISTS MATE 3/C	1	(1)

PILOT	2	
PILOT 1/c	1	
QUARTERGUNNER	10	(1)
QUARTERMASTER	40	
QUARTERMASTER 2/C	1	
QUARTERMASTER 3/C	2	
RADIO ELECTRICIAN	1	(1)
SAILMAKERS MATE	2	
SEAMAN	114	(1)
SEAMAN 1/C	3	(2)
SEAMAN APPRENTICE 2c	1	
SHELL MAN	1	
SHIPFITTER 1/C	2	
ENGINEERS COOK	1	
SHIPS COOK	2	
SHIPS COOK 1/C	2	
SHIPS COOK 3/C	1	
SHIPS CORPORAL	1	
SHIPS PRINTER	1	
SIGNAL QUARTERMASTER	5	
SURGEON	2	
TORPEDOMAN 1/C	1	
TORPEDOMAN 2/C	1	
WATERTENDER	8	
WATERTENDER 1/C	1	(1)
YOEMAN	2	
TOTAL	740*	(52)

*Three Navy double recipients earned awards at two different ranks and are counted under each rank-John Cooper as Coxswain and Quartermaster, John Lafferty/Laverty as Fireman and Fireman First Class (1/c) and John McCloy as Coxswain and Chief Boatswain.

U.S. MARINE CORPS

MAJOR GENERAL	1
COLONEL	2

LT. COLONEL	5	(2)
MAJOR	10	(2)
CAPTAIN	24	(4)
1st LIEUTENANT	19	(10)
2nd LIEUTENANT	10	(6)
FIRST SERGEANT	1	
GUNNERY SERGEANT	7	(3)
ORDERLY SERGEANT	3	
STAFF SERGEANT	14	(8)
TECHNICAL SERGEANT	1	
SERGEANT	38	(17)
CORPORAL	38	(16)
LANCE CORPORAL	14	(13)
PRIVATE FIRST CLASS	48	(41)
PRIVATE	59	(6)
DRUMMER	1	
TOTAL	**295***	**(128)**

*One Marine, Dan Daly, received two Medals in separate wars. One was as a Private and the other was as a Gunnery Sergeant. He is included under both ranks.

U.S. AIR FORCE

COLONEL	1	(1)
LT. COLONEL	1	
MAJOR	6	(3)
CAPTAIN	6	(4)
1ST LIEUTENANT	1	
AIRMAN FIRST CLASS	2	(1)
TOTAL	**17**	**(9)**

U.S. COAST GUARD

SIGNALMAN FIRST CLASS	1	(1)

ALL AWARDS
TOTAL AWARDS LIVING AND (POSTHUMOUS) BY SERVICE:

ARMY	2,400 (424)
MARINES	296 (128)
NAVY	745 (52)
AIR FORCE	17 (9)
COAST GUARD	1 (1)
TOTAL	**3,459 (614)**

ALL AWARDS BY LOCATION OF ACTION:

Since 1862, a total of 3,459 Medals of Honor have been awarded for actions on land, in the air and in the contiguous waters of 36 American states, the District of Columbia, 33 foreign countries, 24 Pacific islands, 2 Atlantic islands, 2 oceans, 4 seas, 1 channel, 1 gulf and 1 of the poles.

Two have been awarded for general meritorious services throughout a military career, a dozen have been awarded for actions in multiple locations (more than one state or country) and 137 of them do not have a location noted in the citation.

In a testament to the violence and divisiveness of our own Civil War, more have been awarded within our own borders than in foreign conflicts. More have been awarded for actions in states bordering our national capital than in World War II and Vietnam combined.

Alabama	119
Arizona	140
Arkansas	10
California	15
Colorado	12
Connecticut	1
Delaware	2
Delaware River	1
District of Columbia	4
Florida	11
Georgia	84
Hawaii	17
Idaho	4
Kansas	16
Kansas/Colorado	1
Kentucky	3
Louisiana	58
Massachusetts	1
Maryland	29
Minnesota	1

Mississippi	155
Missouri	7
Montana	91
Nebraska	14
New Mexico	18
New York	9
North Carolina	112
Oklahoma (Indian Territory)	1
Oregon	1
Pennsylvania	66
Rhode Island	7
South Carolina	32
South Dakota	30
Tennessee	104
Texas	69
Utah	1
Virginia	693
West Virginia	5
Wyoming	4

TOTAL WITHIN THE U.S.   1948

Atlantic Ocean	14
Attu Island	1
Belgium	20
Bougainville Island	5
Brazil	4
Burma	1
Cambodia	2
Canada	1
Caribbean Sea	3
Chile	3
China	62
Cuba	104
Dominican Republic	3
Egypt	2
English Channel	17
Eniwetok Island	1

France	186
Germany	59
Greenland	1
Guadalcanal	10
Guam	4
Gulf of Mexico	4
Haiti	8
Holland	3
Italy	68
Iwo Jima	27
Japan	4
Korea	146
Laos	6
Liberia	2
Los Negros Island	1
Luxembourg	2
Makin Island	1
Mediterranean Sea	2
Mexico	61
Midway Island	2
Minorca	1
Morocco	3
Namur Island	3
Netherlands East Indies	1
New Britain	3
New Guinea	11
Nicaragua	8
North Pole	2
North Vietnam	9
Okinawa	24
Over Europe	5
Pacific Ocean	20
Peleliu	8
Peru	4
Philippine Islands	143
Portugal	2
Roi Island	1
Rumania	7

Saipan	7
Samoa	1
Savo Island	4
Sea of Marmora	1
Sicily	5
Solomon Islands	15
Somalia	2
South China Sea	1
South Vietnam	228
Tarawa	4
Tinian	2
Truk Island	1
Tunisia	3
Uruguay	2
Wake Island	1

TOTAL OUTSIDE THE U.S 1360

General Service	2
Multiple Locations	12
Unknown Location	137

TOTAL 151

GRAND TOTAL 3459

CRUNCHING THE NUMBERS

It is difficult to pick up any two volumes giving tabulations of Medal of Honor awards and find the same answer to some seemingly simple questions like "How many Medals have been awarded" and "How many Medal recipients have there been?" The accuracy problems have primarily been caused by confusion from three sources. First is the double recipients, some for the same action, some for separate actions, some in one conflict and some in separate conflicts. Second is the extended delays in awarding retroactive awards. Third is the rescinding of many awards by a committee in 1917 and the decades-later restoration of some of those awards. These factors create an inherent imbalance in the number of individual recipients compared to the number of awards.

George Lang, M.H. (himself a Vietnam MOH recipient), Raymond L. Collins and Gerard F. White published their two-volume MEDAL OF HONOR RECIPIENTS 1863-1994 in 1995. In it, they assign a separate number to each Medal recipient with some notable exceptions. The difficulties caused by the exceptions are easily overcome when compared to the depth and breadth of their comprehensive research.

Among the many other clarifications they are responsible for is the discovery that one previously believed double award recipient (Army Corporal/Sergeant Patrick Leonard in the Indian Campaigns) was shown to be two separate men. Conversely, they have balanced the scales by discovering a previously unknown double recipient. Navy Fireman John Lafferty (Civil War) and Navy First Class Fireman John Laverty (Interim 1871-98) were shown to be the same person. Therefore we are still left with 19 double recipients.

Lang, Collins and White ended up with 3,399 sequentially numbered recipients. Even as timely as their volumes were, they still couldn't keep up with the system. President Clinton has awarded 35 more Medals since their publication was printed, 30 for actions in World War II, three for Vietnam and one each for the Spanish-American War and the Civil War (see Most Recent Awards). President George W. Bush has awarded four Medals, one for World War II and three for Vietnam.

The issue was somewhat further clouded by the fact that they assigned one number to the 12 recipients who earned both of their Medals in the same conflict and two separate numbers to the 7 who earned them in separate conflicts. They also didn't assign numbers to the nine Unknown Soldiers. Even so, their tabulation helps arrive at some more accurate numbers.

By taking their base number (3,399), adding the 12 extra awards of the dozen double recipients listed under a single number, 39 new awards and the nine Unknown Soldiers, we arrive at a total of 3,459 awards.

Similarly, by taking their base number (3,399), subtracting the second awards of the seven double recipients listed under separate numbers and adding the 39 new awards and the nine Unknown Soldiers, we arrive at a total of 3,440 individual award recipients.

AS OF JANUARY 21, 2004:

TOTAL NUMBER OF MEDALS AWARDED	3,459
TOTAL NUMBER OF MEDAL RECIPIENTS (1 woman)	3,440
TOTAL NUMBER OF POSTHUMOUS AWARDS	614
TOTAL NUMBER OF OFFICERS	781
TOTAL NUMBER OF ENLISTED MEN	2,642
TOTAL NUMBER OF CIVILIANS	8
TOTAL NUMBER OF UNKNOWN RANK	9
TOTAL NUMBER OF DOUBLE RECIPIENTS	19

(14 men received two Medals of Honor for separate actions and 5 Marines received double awards in World War I).

Name Errors

The names on many Medal of Honor citations are not the true names of the recipients including three men who were double recipients. There are two basic reasons for this. One is that the name is misspelled because of phonetics, a lack of literacy, or the confusion caused by names of other than Anglo-Saxon origin, or through the use of a middle name or nickname as the primary name. The other reason is because the person originally used a false name on their military records for some personal reason. A third and much more infrequent reason is because the person legally changed their name after the award.

As might be expected, the farther back in time, the more frequent these errors occur. The errors decrease in more modern times with better birth records and the increasing emphasis on accurate identification. For these reasons, these types of errors have virtually stopped since World War II. The following list shows the errors in these two categories for each conflict and the true names of the citations under false names.

CIVIL WAR:

| Misspelled | 62 |
| False Names | 17 |

Name on Citation	True Name
Richard Binder	Richard Bigle
John Brown	Thomas Hayes
John Chapman	Charles F. Kaufman
Robert T. Clifford	Robert T. Kelley
John Cooper	John Laver Mather
Robert Graham	Frederick Hall
Harry Harvey	Harry Huckman
James Howard	James Brown
Martin Howard	Michael C. Horgan
John Mack	Michael Connely
James Madison	James Congdon
Charles Melville	James Ramsbottom
John Miller	Henry Fey
James H. Morgan	James H. Creevey
John Rush	Israel W. Little
George Taylor	George Taylor Johnson
Henry A. Thompson	Roderick P. Connelly

INDIAN CAMPAIGNS:

Misspelled	24
False Names	11

Name on Citation	True Name
James Anderson	James Smyth
John B. Babcock	John Breckinridge
Clay Beauford	Welford Chapman Bridwell
Charles Gardner	Simon Suhler
Fred Stewart Hay	Frederick H. Schwabe
Charles H. Montrose	Alexander D. Munson
John Mott	John Mott McMahan
Theodore Ragnar	Ragnar T. Ling-Vannerus
John Tracy	Henry G. Nabers
William Wallace	John A. Wallace
John Ward	John Warrior

NOTE: In addition, there were also Medals awarded to the following Indian Scouts, 10 Apaches and one Pawnee. Because of the language barrier, it is doubtful if some of the names on the citations are their true given names. On only one do we have a clue as to his true name. The citations are listed under: Blanquet, Chiquito Co-Rux-Te-Cod-Ish (see in that section), Elsatsoosh, Jim, Kelsay, Kosoha, Machol, Nannasaddie, Nantaje (Nantahe), and Rowdy.

KOREAN CAMPAIGN (1871):

Misspelled	1

INTERIM 1871-98:

Misspelled	3
False Names	2

Name on Citation	True Name
George Low	George L. Evatt
Louis Williams	Ludwig Andreas Olsen

SPANISH-AMERICAN WAR:

Misspelled	2
False Names	1

Name on Citation	True Name
James Meredith	Patrick F. Ford Jr.

BOXER REBELLION:

Misspelled	1
False Names	3

Name on Citation	True Name
Harry Fisher	Franklin J. Phillips
Henry W. Davis	William Henry Murray
Francis Thomas Ryan	Frank Gallagher

HAITIAN CAMPAIGN(1915):

False Names	1

Name on Citation	True Name
Samuel Gross	Samuel Marguilies

NICARAGUAN CAMPAIGN:

Name Change	1

Name on Citation	True Name
Donald L. Truesdell	Donald L. Truesdale

WORLD WAR I:

Misspelled	1
False Names	2

Name on Citation	True Name
Jake Allex	Jake Allex Mandushich
Charles F. Hoffman	Ernest August Janson

Name Change	1

Ludovicus Van Iersel	Louis Van Iersel

WORLD WAR II:

Name Change	1

Name on Citation	True Name
Christos H. Karaberis	Chris Carr

TOTALS:

Misspelled	94
False Names	37
Name Changes	3

Places Of Burial

One of the benefits extended to Medal of Honor recipients is the right to a funeral with full military honors and burial in a national military cemetery including those at the various service academies. Most Medal recipients or their families still opt for private or family cemeteries but many recipients have availed themselves of this right. The following list shows the most frequent or notable places of burial of Medal of Honor recipients. It should be noted that the places of burial for all Medal recipients are not known. Therefore these numbers cannot be considered to be precise but must be considered as a minimum.

CIVIL WAR:

Arlington National Cemetery, Washington, D.C	95
U.S. Military Academy, West Point, New York	9
Fort Leavenworth, Kansas, National Cemetery	5
Bath National Cemetery, Bath, New York	5
Cypress Hills National Cemetery, Brooklyn, N.Y	5
Hampton Roads National Cemetery, Virginia	5
Los Angeles National Cemetery, California	5
San Francisco National Cemetery, California	4
Chattanooga National Cemetery, Tennessee	4
San Antonio National Cemetery, Texas	1
U.S. Naval Academy, Annapolis, Maryland	1

INDIAN CAMPAIGNS:

Arlington National Cemetery	34
Soldiers Home National Cemetery, Washington DC	19
San Francisco National Cemetery, California	11
San Antonio National Cemetery, Texas	10
Custer Battlefield National Cemetery, Montana	6
U.S. Military Academy, West Point, New York	2

INTERIM
1866-70:

Cypress Hills National Cemetery, Brooklyn, N.Y.	1

KOREA CAMPAIGN
1871:

Cypress Hills National Cemetery, Brooklyn, N.Y.	1
Los Angeles National Cemetery, California	1

INTERIM
1871-98:

Arlington National Cemetery	3
Long Island National Cemetery, New York	2
Cypress Hills National Cemetery, Brooklyn, N.Y.	1

SPANISH-AMERICAN WAR:

Arlington National Cemetery	17
San Francisco National Cemetery, California	3
U.S. Military Academy, West Point	2
U.S. Naval Academy, Annapolis	2
Fort Leavenworth National Cemetery, Kansas	1
Fort Rosecrans Natl. Cem., San Diego, Calif	1
Long Island National Cemetery, New York	1
Cypress Hills National Cemetery, Brooklyn, N.Y.	1
San Antonio National Cemetery, Texas	1

PHILIPPINE INSURRECTION:

Arlington National Cemetery	26
San Francisco National Cemetery, California	6
Soldiers Home National Cemetery, Washington DC	1
Long Island National Cemetery, New York	1
Fort Leavenworth National Cemetery, Kansas	1
Los Angeles National Cemetery, California	1

BOXER REBELLION:

Arlington National Cemetery	14
San Francisco National Cemetery, California	3
Cypress Hills National Cemetery, Brooklyn, N.Y.	3
Natl. Memorial Cem. of the Pacific, Honolulu	1
Los Angeles National Cemetery, California	1

INTERIM
1899-1910:

Arlington National Cemetery	9
Long Island National Cemetery, New York	3
Golden Gate National Cemetery, San Francisco	2
Cypress Hills National Cemetery, Brooklyn, N.Y	2
Fort Rosecrans Natl. Cem., San Diego, Calif	1
San Francisco National Cemetery, California	1

VERA CRUZ CAMPAIGN:

Arlington National Cemetery	39
Fort Rosecrans Natl. Cem., San Diego, Calif	5
U.S. Naval Academy, Annapolis	2
Long Island National Cemetery, New York	1
San Francisco National Cemetery, California	1

HAITIAN CAMPAIGN
1915:

Arlington National Cemetery	1
U.S. Naval Academy, Annapolis	1
Cypress Hills National Cemetery, Brooklyn, N.Y	1
Fort Rosecrans Natl. Cem., San Diego, Calif	1

INTERIM
1915-16:

Arlington National Cemetery	3
Cypress Hills National Cemetery, Brooklyn, N.Y	2

NICARAGUAN CAMPAIGN:

Arlington National Cemetery	1

WORLD WAR I:

Arlington National Cemetery	25
Meuse Argonne Battlefield Cemetery, France	8
Somme Battlefield Cemetery, France	3
Long Island National Cemetery, New York	2
Fort Rosecrans Natl. Cem., San Diego, Calif	2
Cypress Hills National Cemetery, Brooklyn, N.Y	1
San Francisco National Cemetery, California	1
San Antonio National Cemetery, Texas	1

HAITIAN CAMPAIGN
1919-20:

Fort Rosecrans Natl. Cem., San Diego, Calif	1

INTERIM
1920-40:

Arlington National Cemetery	7
San Francisco National Cemetery, California	1

WORLD WAR II:

Arlington National Cemetery	51
Natl. Memorial Cem. of the Pacific, Honolulu	29
AMBC National Cemetery, Manila, Philippines	27
Golden Gate National Cemetery, San Francisco	5
Long Island National Cemetery, New York	5
Fort Rosecrans Natl. Cem., San Diego, Calif	3
U.S. Military Academy, West Point	1
U.S. Naval Academy, Annapolis	1
Los Angeles National Cemetery, California	1

KOREAN WAR:

Natl. Memorial Cem. of the Pacific, Honolulu	15
Arlington National Cemetery	15
San Francisco National Cemetery, California	3
Fort Rosecrans Natl. Cem., San Diego, Calif	1
Long Island National Cemetery, New York	1
U.S. Military Academy, West Point	1

VIETNAM WAR:

Arlington National Cemetery	18
Long Island National Cemetery, New York	4
Fort Rosecrans Natl. Cem., San Diego, Calif	4
Natl. Memorial Cem. of the Pacific, Honolulu	3
Golden Gate National Cemetery, San Francisco	2
U.S. Military Academy, West Point	1

TOTALS (as of March 2002):

Arlington National Cemetery	372
Natl. Memorial Cem. of the Pacific, Honolulu	48
San Francisco National Cemetery, California	34
AMBC National Cemetery, Manila, Philippines	27
Long Island National Cemetery, New York	20
Soldiers Home National Cemetery, Washington DC	20
Fort Rosecrans Natl. Cem., San Diego, Calif.	19
Cypress Hills National Cemetery, Brooklyn, N.Y.	18
U.S. Military Academy, West Point	16
San Antonio National Cemetery, Texas	13
Los Angeles National Cemetery, California	9
Golden Gate National Cemetery, San Francisco	9
Meuse Argonne Battlefield Cemetery, France	8
U.S. Naval Academy, Annapolis	7
Fort Leavenworth National Cemetery, Kansas	7

MEDAL PRESENTATIONS

Information on when, where and by whom Medals of Honor have been presented to recipients was sketchy at best for the first five decades of its existence. In fact, it was not until after World War I that information has been made available on more than half of the presentations in any given conflict or period. The following lists document what information is available on who presented the Medals to the recipients (or their families in the case of posthumous awards) in each conflict. It should be noted that due to extensive delays in awarding some Medals, some presentations were made by Presidents and other officials who served long after the conflict for which the award was made.

CIVIL WAR

The first six Medals presented were to Army enlisted men involved in "The Great Locomotive Chase". They were presented by Secretary of War Edwin M. Stanton on March 25, 1863, and the men were then permitted "a short visit" with President Lincoln. Throughout the remainder of the war, presentations were probably made by unit commanders or ship's captains. The following individuals presented Medals:

6   Secretary of War Edwin M. Stanton
9   Presented to sailors by the Captain of the U.S.S. *Agawam* on May 12, 1865, for the battle of Fort Fisher, North Carolina.
6   Presented by other ships captains to five sailors and one Marine in individual ceremonies aboard various ships.
1   by President Abraham Lincoln.
1   by President Ulysses S. Grant.
1   by Assistant Secretary of War Doe.
1   by a Massachusetts veterans organization in 1897.
1   by President William J. Clinton.

INDIAN CAMPAIGNS:

8   by Colonel Randal MacKenzie, Commander, 4th U.S. Cavalry. (A ninth award was presented posthumously for the same action.)

INTERIM 1871-98:

3 by Navy Lt. Commander Theodore F. Jewell.
1 by President Theodore Roosevelt.

SPANISH-AMERICAN WAR:

1 by President Theodore Roosevelt.
1 by President Franklin D. Roosevelt.
1 by President William J. Clinton.

PHILIPPINE INSURRECTION:

4 by President William Howard Taft
2 by President Franklin D. Roosevelt.
1 by President Woodrow Wilson.

BOXER REBELLION:

1 by the (unnamed) Captain of the USS Brooklyn.

INTERIM 1899-1910:

1 by President Warren G. Harding.

ACTIONS AGAINST PHILIPPINE OUTLAWS (1911):

1 by the wife of commanding officer Major General J. Franklin Bell.

VERA CRUZ:

1 by President Calvin Coolidge.
1 by President William Howard Taft.

HAITIAN CAMPAIGN
(1915):

1   by Marine Corps Commandant Major General George Barnett.

WORLD WAR I:

10   by General John J. Pershing.
3   by President Herbert Hoover.
1   President Franklin D. Roosevelt
1   President George Bush
1   Under Secretary of the Navy Franklin D. Roosevelt
1   General William R. Smith
1   Major General Duncan (82nd Infantry Division)
1   Brigadier General Hickok
1   Admiral N.A. McCully
1   Admiral William A. Moffett

HAITIAN CAMPAIGN
(1919-20):

2   by Marine General John A. Lejeune.

SECOND NICARAGUAN CAMPAIGN:

1   by Marine Brigadier General Randolph C. Berkeley.

INTERIM
1920-40:

7   by President Calvin Coolidge.
4   by Secretary of the Navy Charles Edison.
1   by Marine Brigadier General Harry Lee.

WORLD WAR II:

86 by President Harry S. Truman
30 by President William J. Clinton
27 by President Franklin D. Roosevelt
13 by Army Lt. General Alexander M. Patch III
7   by Army General Mark W. Clark
5   by Secretary of the Navy James V. Forrestal
4   by Marine General Alexander A. Vandegrift
3   by Army General Douglas MacArthur
3   by Army Lt. General Jacob L. Devers
3   by Navy Admiral Chester Nimitz
2   by President Jimmy Carter
2   by Secretary of War Henry L. Stimson
2   by Army General George S. Patton
2   by Army Air Corps Lt. General Carl A. Spaatz
2   by Army Lt. General O.W. Griswold
2   by Army Major General Lunsford E. Oliver
2   by Army Major General Terry Allen
2   by Army Major General Sherman Miles
2   by Navy Rear Admiral A.C. Bennett
1   by President Ronald Reagan
1   by President George W. Bush
1   by Vice President Richard M. Nixon
1   by Army General George C. Marshall
1   by Army General Harry Collins
1   byArmy General George C. Kenney
1   by Army Air Corps General Henry H. Arnold
1   by Army Air Corps General Curtis Lemay
1   by Army Air Corps General Ira Eaker
1   by Navy Admiral Ernest J. King
1   by Army Lt. General Leonard Derow
1   by Army Lt. General Millard F. Harmon
1   by Army Lt. General John C.H. Lee
1   by Army Lt. General Geoffrey Keyes
1   by Army Lt. General Clarence R. Hubner
1   by Navy Vice Admiral Thomas C. Kincaid
1   by Navy Vice Admiral Ephraim P. Holmes

1   by Navy Vice Admiral A.S. Carpender
1   by Navy Vice Admiral John W. Greensale
1   by Army Major General H.C. Pratt
1   by Army Major General Leland S. Hobbs
1   by Army Major General Frederick Halslip
1   by Army Major General Jonathan W. Anderson
1   by Army Major General C.L. Scott
1   by Army Major General Henry Terrell Jr.
1   by Army Major General Leonard F. Wing
1   by Army Major General Francis B. Melon
1   by Army Major General James Van Fleet III
1   by Army Major General Bruce Magruder
1   by Army Air Corps Major General Walter H. Frank
1   by Army Air Corps Major General James P. Hodges
1   by Army Air Corps Major General Ennis C. Whitehead
1   by Army Air Corps Major General Barton K. Yount
1   by Army Air Corps Major General Ralph P. Cousins
1   by Army Air Corps Major General Lewis H. Brereton
1   by Navy Rear Admiral J.A. Taffinder
1   by Navy Rear Admiral Royal E. Ingersoll
1   by Navy Rear Admiral Joseph J. Clark
1   by Marine Major General Joseph C. Fegan
1   by Marine Major General Ralph Mitchell
1   by Marine Major General Lewis G. Merritt
1   by Army Brigadier General Ralph K. Robertson
1   by Army Brigadier General Robert M. Hardaway
1   by Army Brigadier General E.F. Koenig
1   by Army Brigadier General Frank L. Culin Jr.
1   by Army Brigadier General Frank Dorn
1   by Army General Danielson
1   by Army Colonel A.E. Merrill
1   by Marine Colonel Norman E. True
1   by Minister of Australia Nelson Trussler Johnson

KOREAN WAR:

27 by President Harry S. Truman
18 by Army General Omar Bradley
14 by President Dwight David Eisenhower
10 by Secretary of the Army Robert Lovett
10 by Secretary of the Navy Dan A. Kimball
5 by Vice President Richard M. Nixon
3 by Under Secretary of the Army Earl D. Johnson
3 by Under Secretary of the Navy Francis P. Whitehair
2 by Secretary of the Navy Robert B. Anderson
1 by Secretary of the Army Robert T. Stevens
1 by Secretary of the Navy Charles S. Thomas
1 by Secretary of the Air Force Talbott
1 by Air Force General Hoyt S. Vandenberg
1 by Air Force General Nathan F. Twining
1 by Navy Rear Admiral John H. Brown Jr.

VIETNAM WAR:

104 by President Richard M. Nixon
38 by President Lyndon B. Johnson
38 by Vice President Spiro T. Agnew
19 by Secretary of the Army Stanley R. Resor
14 by Vice President Gerald Ford
10 by Secretary of the Navy Paul R. Ignatius
6 by President Gerald Ford
3 by President William J. Clinton
3 by President George W. Bush
2 by President Ronald Reagan
2 by Secretary of the Navy Paul H. Nitze
1 by Secretary of the Navy Edward Hidalgo
1 by Secretary of the Navy W. Graham Claytor Jr.
1 by Secretary of the Air Force Harold Brown
1 by an unnamed Under Secretary of the Navy
1 by General Donley P. Bolton

SOMALIA:

2   by President William J. Clinton

UNKNOWN SOLDIERS—-

1   by President Warren Harding (World War I)
2   by President Dwight D. Eisenhower (World War II and Korea)
1   by President Ronald Reagan (Vietnam)

MOST AWARDS PRESENTED:

Harry S. Truman	113	(as President)
Richard M. Nixon	110	(as President and Vice President)
Lyndon B. Johnson	38	(as President)
Spiro T. Agnew	38	(as Vice President)
William J. Clinton	37	(as President)
Franklin D. Roosevelt	31	(as President and Under Secretary of the Navy)
Gerald Ford	20	(as President and Vice President)

Among the unusual circumstances involving the presentations of Medals of Honor are the following:

Marine Major Gregory "Pappy" Boyington was recommended for the Medal for shooting down 26 Japanese planes between September 12 and January 3, 1944, in the South Pacific. He was shot down and captured before he could receive the Medal. It was presented to his mother in March 1944 by President Roosevelt. He survived the war in a prison camp and when he returned home, his Medal was presented to him personally by President Truman on October 5, 1945.

Army Private William John Crawford was recommended for the Medal for his actions in Italy on September 13, 1943. When it was approved the next year, he was missing in action and presumed dead. The Medal was posthumously presented to his father on May 11, 1944, by Army Major General Terry Allen. Crawford survived the war and returned home but his Medal was never formally presented to him until May 30, 1984, when President Ronald Reagan made the presentation while Crawford was a janitor at the U.S. Air Force Academy in Colorado Springs, Colorado.

Army Sergeant Kenneth E. Gruennert was posthumously awarded the Medal for heroism on New Guinea on December 24, 1942. When invited to the White House to have the Medal presented to them by President Roosevelt, Gruennert's parents declined with a polite letter, saying that they felt their trip would be an unnecessary expenditure of government funds and would detract from the war effort. At their wishes, their dead son's Medal of Honor was sent to them through the U.S. Mail along with a letter from the Secretary of War stating that "We stand humble in the face of such a demonstration of patriotism as yours.

"Navy Chief Watertender Peter Tomich was posthumously awarded the Medal for heroism during the sinking of the battleship U.S.S. *Utah* at Pearl Harbor on December 7, 1941. A native of Austria, Tomich had no living relatives to receive the Medal so when the Navy named a destroyer after him, his Medal was presented to the ship by Rear Admiral Monroe Kelly. When the U.S.S. *Tomich* was decommissioned on September 20, 1946, the Medal was returned to the Navy Department. On May 25, 1947, Utah Governor Herbert B. Maw made Tomich an honorary citizen of Utah, the state for which his battleship was named. Tomich's Medal was presented to the State of Utah in the state capitol by Rear Admiral Mahlon S. Tisdale.

The Medal As A Path To Promotion

This section deals solely with the advancement of Medal of Honor recipients in the military although many others who chose not to make a career of the service succeeded in other areas such as business, education and politics. One became President and many others became senators, congressmen, governors or held lesser elected offices.

There are two primary arguments here. One is that the military tends to promote their Medal of Honor recipients faster and farther as a result of their having received the Medal. Another is that the basic qualities necessary for earning the Medal (leadership, courage, initiative, independence of thought and action, combat expertise and others) lend themselves more to these promotional opportunities. I would tend to favor the latter argument although there have doubtlessly been examples of both arguments applied in real life.

The fact is many Medal of Honor recipients were promoted after their Medal-winning actions, not necessarily immediately afterwards or as a result of the action but eventually, some higher than others. This is to be expected to some degree simply because, once recognized, the recognition of the qualities necessary to earn the Medal would probably continue to be exercised, making the person a valuable military asset and obviously capable of accepting more authority and responsibility.

One of the rarer but time-honored traditions of the American military is the so-called "mustang", a soldier who starts at the bottom of the ladder, learns his soldiering craft by working his way up through the enlisted ranks and is eventually commissioned as an officer. A much larger than average percentage of Medal recipients made the transition from enlisted to commissioned status. An even smaller percentage progress from the enlisted ranks to the ultimate commissioned status, that of General officer or, in the Navy, flag rank, i.e. Admiral.

In their two-volume work, Lang, Collins and White included the highest rank achieved by as many Medal recipients as they could determine. It would be naive to expect these results to be comprehensive or perfectly accurate in all cases but their research is extensive and instructive. Without adjusting the numbers to account for double Medal recipients, the results of an examination of them are as follows:

CIVIL WAR:

ARMY

1,167 individuals received non-posthumous awards.
595 received promotions afterwards.
161 enlisted men were commissioned as officers.
88 progressed to general officer rank.
1 attained general officer from enlisted rank

NAVY

305 individuals received non-posthumous awards.
61 received promotions afterwards.
   None progressed from enlisted to commissioned status nor to admiral rank.

MARINES

17 individuals received non-posthumous awards.
1 received a promotion afterwards.
   None progressed from enlisted to commissioned status or to general officer rank.

NON-COMBAT
1865-71:

ARMY

1 individual received a non-posthumous award.
    He was not promoted.

NAVY

13 individuals received non-posthumous awards.
1 received a promotion afterwards.
1 enlisted man was commissioned as a officer.
    None progressed to admiral rank.

INDIAN CAMPAIGNS:

ARMY

411 individuals received non-posthumous awards.
144 received a promotion afterwards.
10 enlisted men were commissioned as officers.
21 progressed to general officer rank.

KOREAN CAMPAIGN
(1871):

NAVY

9 individuals received non-posthumous awards.
2 received a promotion afterwards.
None were commissioned as officers or progressed to admiral rank.

MARINES

6 individuals received non-posthumous awards.
None were promoted.

NON-COMBAT 1871-1898:

NAVY

101 individuals received non-posthumous awards.
8 received a promotion afterwards.
1 enlisted man was commissioned as an officer.

MARINES

2 individuals received non-posthumous awards.
1 received a promotion afterwards.

SPANISH-AMERICAN WAR:

ARMY

30 individuals received non-posthumous awards.
19 received a promotion afterwards.
1 enlisted man was commissioned as an officer.
3 progressed to general officer rank.

NAVY

64 individuals received non-posthumous awards.
35 received a promotion afterwards.
6 enlisted men were commissioned as officers.
1 progressed to admiral rank.

MARINES

15 individuals received non-posthumous awards.
11 received a promotion afterwards.
1 enlisted man was commissioned as an officer.

SAMOAN CAMPAIGN:

NAVY

1 individual received a non-posthumous award.
  He was not promoted.

MARINES

3 individuals received non-posthumous awards.
1 received a promotion afterwards.
1 enlisted man was commissioned as an officer.

PHILIPPINE INSURRECTION
(1899-1902):

ARMY

65 individuals received non-posthumous awards.
40 received promotions afterwards.
8 enlisted men were commissioned as officers.
8 progressed to general officer rank.

NAVY

5 individuals received non-posthumous awards.
2 received promotions afterwards.

MARINES

6 individuals received non-posthumous awards.
6 received promotions afterwards.
1 enlisted man was commissioned as an officer.
2 progressed to general officer rank.

BOXER REBELLION:

ARMY

4 individuals received non-posthumous awards.
4 received promotions afterwards.
1 enlisted man was commissioned as an officer.
1 progressed to general officer rank.

NAVY

22 individuals received non-posthumous awards.
12 received promotions afterwards.
6 enlisted men were commissioned as officers.

MARINES

32 individuals received non-posthumous awards.
16 received promotions afterwards.
3 enlisted men were commissioned as officers.

NON-COMBAT
1899-1910:

NAVY

48 individuals received non-Posthumous awards.
15 received promotions afterwards.
8 enlisted men were commissioned as officers.

MARINES

2 individuals received non-posthumous awards.
    None were promoted.

PHILIPPINE ACTIONS AGAINST OUTLAWS:

ARMY

1 individual received a non-posthumous award.
    He was not promoted.

NAVY

5 individuals received non-posthumous awards.
1 received a promotion afterwards.

VERA CRUZ:

ARMY

1 individual received a non-posthumous award.
1 received a promotion afterwards.

NAVY

46 individuals received non-posthumous awards.
37 received a promotion afterwards.
8 enlisted men were commissioned as officers.
16 progressed to admiral rank.

MARINES

9 individuals received non-posthumous awards.
9 received a promotion afterwards.
8 progressed to general officer rank.

HAITIAN CAMPAIGN
(1915):

MARINES

6 individuals received non-posthumous awards.
5 received a promotion afterwards
3 progressed to general officer rank.

NON-COMBAT
1915-1916:

NAVY

7 individuals received non-posthumous awards.
3 received a promotion afterwards.
1 enlisted man was commissioned as an officer.
2 progressed to admiral rank.

DOMINICAN REPUBLIC:

MARINES

3 individuals received non-posthumous awards.
2 received a promotion afterwards.
1 progressed to general officer rank.

WORLD WAR I:

ARMY

63 individuals received non-posthumous awards.
22 received a promotion afterwards.
  7 enlisted men were commissioned as officers.
  3 progressed to general officer rank.

NAVY

19 individuals received non-posthumous awards.
11 received a promotion afterwards.
  3 enlisted men were commissioned as officers.
  2 progressed to admiral rank.

MARINES

4 individuals received non-posthumous awards.
3 received promotions afterwards.
2 enlisted men were commissioned as officers.

HAITIAN CAMPAIGN
(1919-1920):

MARINES

2 individuals received non-posthumous awards.
1 received a promotion afterwards.
1 progressed to general officer rank

NICARAGUAN CAMPAIGN:

MARINES

2 individuals received non-posthumous awards.
1 enlisted man was commissioned as an officer.
1 progressed to general officer rank.

INTERIM
1920-1940:

ARMY

2 individuals received non-posthumous awards.
1 received a promotion afterwards.
1 progressed to general officer rank.

NAVY

11 individuals received non-posthumous awards.
7 received a promotion afterwards.
4 enlisted men were commissioned as officers.
2 progressed to admiral rank.

MARINES

1 individual received a non-posthumous award.
1 received a promotion afterwards.

WORLD WAR II:

ARMY

142 individuals received non-posthumous awards.
  82 received a promotion afterwards.
  17 enlisted men were commissioned as officers.
   6 progressed to general officer rank.
   2 promotions were posthumous.

NAVY

  25 individuals received non-posthumous awards.
  23 received a promotion afterwards.
   4 enlisted men were commissioned as officers.
   7 progressed to admiral rank.
   2 promotions were posthumous.

MARINES

  31 individuals received non-posthumous awards.
  27 received a promotion afterwards.
   5 enlisted men were commissioned as officers.
   7 progressed to general officer rank.
   1 promotion was posthumous.

KOREAN WAR:

ARMY

21 individuals received non-posthumous awards.
16 received a promotion afterwards.
  4 enlisted men were commissioned as officers.
  2 promotions were posthumous.

NAVY

  2 individuals received non-posthumous awards.
  2 received a promotion afterwards.

MARINES

14 individuals received non-posthumous awards.
10 received a promotion afterwards.
  2 enlisted men were commissioned as officers.
  1 progressed to general officer rank.

AIR FORCE

No individuals received a non-posthumous award.
1 received a promotion afterwards.
1 promotion was posthumous.

VIETNAM WAR:

ARMY

60 individuals received non-posthumous awards.
49 received a promotion afterwards.
 5 enlisted men were commissioned as officers.
 3 progressed to general officer rank.
 1 promotion was posthumous.

NAVY

10 individuals received non-posthumous awards.
 7 received a promotion afterwards.
 2 enlisted men were commissioned as officers.
 1 progressed to admiral rank.

MARINES

13 individuals received non-posthumous awards.
12 received a promotion afterwards.
 1 progressed to general officer rank.
 1 promotion was posthumous.

AIR FORCE

 8 individuals received non-posthumous awards
 8 received a promotion afterwards.

TOTALS:

ARMY

1976 individuals received awards non-posthumously.
373 received promotions.
214 enlisted men were commissioned as officers.
134 progressed to general officer rank.
1 attained general officer rank from enlisted status.
5 received promotions posthumously.

NAVY

693 individuals received awards non-posthumously.
227 received promotions.
44 enlisted men were commissioned as officers.
31 progressed to admiral rank.
2 received promotions posthumously.

MARINES

168 individuals received awards non-posthumously.
105 received promotions.
15 enlisted men were commissioned as officers.
25 progressed to general officer rank.
2 received promotions posthumously.

AIR FORCE

8 individuals received awards non-posthumously.
8 received promotions
1 received a promotion posthumously.

GRAND TOTALS:

2826 individuals received awards non-posthumously.
715 received promotions.
273 enlisted men were commissioned as officers.
186 progressed to general or admiral rank.
10 received promotions posthumously.
2 attained general officer rank from enlisted status.

There are, of course, many other factors not accounted for in this analysis; the size of the standing military at the time, the size of the individual conflict, increases or reductions in the military manpower, the presence or absence of the draft and others. Also these numbers have not been adjusted to account for civilians or double recipients but are nevertheless instructive.

Another consideration is the fact that a Medal of Honor award to a living, non-disabled recipient may be a considerable inducement to continuing a military career (or, for a draftee, embarking upon one) which would almost inevitably lead to future promotions, with or without the Medal. It is no accident that over half of the 134 currently living Medal of Honor recipients are retired from military careers.

The most rewarding campaign was obviously the Mexican Campaign at Vera Cruz in 1914. Of the 55 Medal of Honor recipients from all services in that campaign, 47 were promoted and 24, almost half of the total, eventually progressed to become either generals or admirals.

ONLY TWO Medal recipients attained general officer rank from an enlisted status, oddly enough at the opposite ends of the Medal's history to date. Daniel Webster Burke earned his Medal at the battle of Antietam in September of 1862. A First Sergeant in the Army at that time, he eventually became a Brigadier General.

James L. Day received his Medal for actions as a Marine Corporal on Okinawa in May of 1945. He eventually retired from the Marine Corps as a Major General before receiving his Medal on July 10, 1998.

Most Recent Awards

CIVIL WAR:

DR. MARY W. WALKER-Dr. Walker's original citation was issued by President Andrew Johnson on November 11, 1865. The review board rescinded her award in 1916 but it was restored by President Jimmy Carter on June 10, 1977.

WILLIAM H WOODALL-Civilian Scout Woodall's original citation was awarded on May 3, 1865, but was rescinded by the review board in 1916. His award was restored in June 1989.

SERGEANT ANDREW JACKSON SMITH-The most recent award of the Medal of Honor for the Civil War was to Andrew Jackson Smith. A black man, Smith was born into slavery about September 3, 1842. He was serving as a Corporal in Company B of the 55th Massachusetts Infantry on November 30, 1864, at the battle of Honey Hill, South Carolina, saving the Union flag from capture after the Color Sergeant was shot. He was promoted to Color Sergeant after the battle. Sgt. Smith was awarded the Medal of Honor posthumously by President Clinton on January 16, 2001, following a petition by his descendants.

INDIAN CAMPAIGNS:

The awards of four civilian scouts for the Army during the Indian Campaigns were rescinded by the review board in 1916. All four awards were restored in June of 1989. They were:

AMOS CHAPMAN
WILLIAM F. CODY
WILLIAM DIXON
JAMES B. DOSHER (DOZIER)

SPANISH AMERICAN WAR:

THEODORE ROOSEVELT-In 1898, Roosevelt resigned as Assistant Secretary of the Navy to accept a Lieutenant Colonel's commission under Colonel Leonard Wood (also a Medal of Honor recipient) and help raise the First Volunteer Cavalry for service in the war. Sent to Cuba, on July 1, Roosevelt, 39, led the famous charge up San Juan Hill which effectively ended the ground war on that island.

Promoted to Colonel, Roosevelt resigned his commission after only five months of service and re-entered politics. He was elected Governor of New York and, two years later, became Vice President under President William McKinley. When McKinley was assassinated in 1901, Roosevelt, at age 42, became the youngest President in United States history on September 14.

On January 16, 2001, he was posthumously awarded the Medal of Honor for his actions. This makes him the only person to hold both the nation's highest office and highest military decoration for valor. This also makes the second father-son team to win the Medal. Arthur MacArthur received the award during the Civil War and his son, Douglas MacArthur, received it during World War II. Roosevelt's son, Theodore Roosevelt Jr., also received the award during World War II for actions on D-Day, June 6, 1944.

WORLD WAR I:

The last Medal of Honor awarded for service in World War I was awarded to Army Corporal **Freddie Stowers**, the only black recipient of that conflict, by President George Bush on April 24, 1991.

WORLD WAR II:

ANTHONY CASAMENTO-Marine Corporal Casamento was awarded his Medal for heroism on Guadalcanal on November 1, 1942. The Medal was belatedly presented to him by President Jimmy Carter on September 12, 1980.

MATT URBAN-Captain Urban was awarded the Medal for multiple acts of heroism in France and Belgium during the summer of 1944. Many of the witnesses to his acts were either killed or captured shortly afterwards. A letter recommending him for the Medal after the war was misplaced in his personnel file. He didn't learn of it until a 9th Infantry Division reunion in 1977. The Medal was presented to him by President Jimmy Carter on July 19, 1980.

FIRST LIEUTENANT VERNON J. BAKER
STAFF SERGEANT EDWARD A. CARTER
FIRST LIEUTENANT JOHN R. FOX
PFC WILLY F. JAMES JR.
STAFF SERGEANT RUBEN RIVERS
CAPTAIN CHARLES L. THOMAS
PRIVATE GEORGE WATSON

These seven awards, the only awards to black servicemen in World War II, were presented by President William Clinton on January 13, 1997. All were posthumous except for Baker.

JAMES L DAY-Marine Corporal Day was awarded the Medal for actions on Okinawa on May 14-17, 1945. In a three-day battle, he suffered multiple wounds while saving the lives of five Marines and killing over 100 enemy soldiers. Remaining in the Marine Corps after the war, he was commissioned as a Lieutenant in Korea and also served in Vietnam. Wounded in all three wars, he received six Purple Hearts. He advanced to the rank of Major General and forbid his men from recommending him for the Medal while he was still on active duty. After his retirement, the Medal was recommended, approved and awarded to him by President William Clinton on January 20, 1998. He died on the following October 28.

STAFF SERGEANT RUDOLPH B. DAVILA
PRIVATE BARNEY F. HAJIRO
PRIVATE SHIZUYA HAYASHI
SECOND LIEUTENANT DANIEL K. INOUYE
TECHNICAL SERGEANT YEIKI KOBASHIGAWA
TECHNICAL SERGEANT YUKIO OKUTSU
PRIVATE GEORGE T. SAKATO
PRIVATE MIKIO HASEMOTO
PRIVATE JOE HAYASHI
STAFF SERGEANT ROBERT T.
PFC KAORU MOTO
PFC KIYOSHI K. MURANAGA
PRIVATE MASATO NAKAE
PRIVATE SHINYEI NAKAMINE
PFC WILLIAM K. NAKAMURA
PFC JOE M. NISHIMOTO
SERGEANT ALLAN M. OHATA
TECHNICAL SERGEANT JAMES K. OKUBO
PFC FRANK H. ONO
STAFF SERGEANT KAZUO OTANI
TECHNICAL SERGEANT TED T. TANOUYE
CAPTAIN FRANCIS B. WAI

In spite of anti-Oriental prejudices rampant following the Japanese attack on Pearl Harbor in 1941, Asian-Pacific Americans were later allowed to serve in the armed services. Two well-known U.S. Army units arose staffed primarily by Americans of Japanese, Chinese, Korean, Filipino and Pacific Island descent—the 100th Infantry Battalion (Separate) and the 442nd Regimental Combat Team.

In spite of their numbers and outstanding service, only two Asia-Pacific Americans were awarded the Medal of Honor during World

War II. In 1996, the Army began reviewing 104 cases where the Distinguished Service Cross (the Army's second highest award for valor in combat) had been awarded to Asia-Pacific Americans in that conflict. Four years later, 22 of those awards were upgraded to the Medal of Honor for the above listed individuals. Nineteen (19) were Japanese Americans, one was Hawaiian/Chinese American and one was Filipino/Spanish/American. All had served in the U.S. Army, the first seven were still living and the remaining 15 were posthumous. All were members of the 100th Infantry Battalion or the 442nd Regimental Combat Team except Davila (7th Infantry Division) and Wai (24th Infantry Division). The awards were presented by President Clinton at the White House on June 21, 2000. The best-known of the recipients was Daniel K. Inouye, Hawaii's first Congressman in 1959 and a U.S. Senator for the previous 38 years.

CAPTAIN BENJAMIN LOUIS SALOMON-Salomon was a dentist serving as the battalion surgeon for the 2nd Battalion, 105th Infantry Regiment, 27th Infantry Division, U.S. Army. During the battle for the island of Saipan on July 7, 1944, Salomon's aid station was caring for numerous casualties when they were overrun by a Japanese human-wave attack. Japanese were bayoneting wounded Americans when Salomon killed several of them. Arranging for the field hospital to be evacuated, he covered their withdrawal with a machine gun until he was slain. The bodies of 98 Japanese soldiers were found around his last position. Captain Salomon was posthumously awarded the Medal of Honor by President George W. Bush on May 1, 2002.

VIETNAM WAR:

DONALD GILBERT COOK-Marine Captain Cook was taken prisoner in Vietnam on December 31, 1964. He remained a prisoner until his death on December 8, 1967. After the war, evidence of his heroic conduct and resistance to the enemy came to light and he was recommended for the Medal of Honor. The posthumous Medal was presented to his family in the Pentagon on May 16, 1980. On March 19, 2003, the Navy destroyer U.S.S. *Donald Cook* was among the first ships to launch Tomahawk missiles into Iraq in Operation Iraqi Freedom.

ROY P. BENVAVIDEZ-Army Special Forces Master Sergeant Benavidez was awarded the Medal for actions while attempting to rescue a surrounded recon team on May 2, 1968. He was belatedly presented his Medal by President Ronald Reagan at the Pentagon on February 24, 1981.

UNKNOWN SOLDIER OF VIETNAM-The Medal of Honor was awarded to the Unknown Soldier of the Vietnam War by President Ronald Reagan on May 28, 1984.

ROBERT R. INGRAM-Navy Petty Officer Ingram served as a Hospital Corpsman with Company C, First Battalion, Seventh Marines in Quang Ngai Province, South Vietnam. During combat on March 28, 1966, he saved a number of Marines while sustaining four wounds. He received his Medal of Honor from President Clinton on July 10, 1998.

ALBERT RASCON -Army Specialist Fourth Class Rascon served as a medic with the Recon Platoon, 1st Battalion, 503rd Infantry, 173rd Airborne Brigade. On March 16, 1966, his unit was ambushed by a large force of Vietnamese. Rascon saved a number of his wounded comrades while sustaining several wounds himself while shielding their bodies from enemy fire and grenade shrapnel. He was recommended for the Medal but the paperwork was lost.

Rascon, born in Mexico in 1945, served a second tour in Vietnam in 1972 as an officer and left the service in 1976 to become an Inspector General with the U.S. Selective Service System. He received his Medal of Honor on February 8, 2000, from President Clinton in a White House ceremony attended by eight of the men he had saved.

WILLIAM H. PITSENBARGER-The second-most recent award for the Vietnam War was made on December 8, 2000, to U.S. Air Force Airman First Class William H. Pitsenbarger. He was a Pararescue man ("PJ"-Parajumper) in the 38th Aerospace Rescue and Recovery Squadron. On April 11, 1966, he went on a rescue mission to recover wounded soldiers of the 1st Infantry Division who were ambushed by a large force near Cam My, 35 miles east of Saigon. Lowered through heavy jungle cover by his helicopter, he rescued wounded and voluntarily remained on the ground to resist the enemy. He was killed by sniper fire before the unit could be relieved. The Air Force awarded only 13 Air Force Crosses (their second-highest decoration) during the Vietnam War. Ten of those were to Pararescue men. Pitsenbarger, 21, was the first man to receive the AFC posthumously on September 22, 1966. Thirty-four years later, enough witnesses were located to justify upgrading his award to the Medal of Honor. He became only the second Air Force enlisted man to receive the award. He was posthumously promoted to Staff Sergeant.

ED W. FREEMAN-On November 14, 1965, Captain Freeman was a helicopter pilot with A Company of the 229th Assault Helicopter Battalion, 1st Cavalry Division. Responding to a surrounded battalion during the battle of the Ia Drang Valley, Captain Freeman flew 14 missions under heavy ground fire to rescue at least 30 wounded men. He was originally awarded the Distinguished Flying Cross but the award was upgraded at the behest of Arizona Senator John McCain, himself a decorated Navy pilot and POW in the Vietnam War. Freeman, 73, was presented his award on July 16, 2001, by President George W. Bush Jr. in the such first award by that President.

CAPTAIN JON EDWARD SWANSON-Captain Swanson was a helicopter pilot with the 1st Troop, 9th Cavalry Squadron, 1st Cavalry Division, U.S. Army. On February 26, 1971, Swanson was participating in an incursion into enemy areas of Cambodia. He repeatedly attacked the enemy, covering the badly outnumbered Americans, until he was shot down. Captain Swanson was posthumously awarded the Medal of Honor on May 1, 2002, by President George W. Bush.

CAPTAIN HUMBERT ROCQUE 'Rocky" VERSACE-Captain Versace, a 1959 West Point graduate, was serving as an advisor to the Military Assistance Advisory Group in the Mekong Delta area of South Vietnam. During a patrol in October of 1963, he was wounded and captured by Viet Cong forces along with two Special Forces soldiers. Adhering strictly to the Code of Conduct, Versace refused to cooperate with his captors, argued with them incessantly, resisted their brainwashing attempts and, in the words of one of his fellow POW's, "told them to go to hell in Vietnamese, French and English." For nearly two years, he organized his fellow POW's, bolstered their morale and endured torture and solitary confinement from his captors. Unable to break his will, the Viet Cong executed him on September 26, 1965. His body was never recovered. Versace was posthumously awarded the Medal of Honor on July 8, 2002, by President George W. Bush.

AND LAST...

Although Medals of Honor were not produced or awarded until the Civil War, the last known surviving veterans of previous wars are as follows;

THE LAST KNOWN SURVIVING VETERAN OF THE AMERICAN REVOLUTION (1775-1784) was Daniel T. Bakeman of Cattaraugas County, New York. He lived to see the United States he helped to free as a teenager tear themselves asunder in civil war and reunite. He died on April 5, 1869, at the age of 109.

THE LAST KNOWN SURVIVING VETERAN OF THE WAR OF 1812 (1812-1815) was Hiram Cronk who died on May 13, 1905, at the age of 105.

THE LAST KNOWN SURVIVING VETERAN OF THE MEXICAN WAR (1846-1848) was Owen Thomas Edgar who died on September 3, 1929, at the age of 98.

THE LAST KNOWN SURVIVING MEDAL RECIPIENT OF THE CIVIL WAR was William H. Sickles of Company B, 7th Wisconsin Infantry, who was born on October 27, 1844. As a 20-year-old Army Sergeant, he earned his Medal at Gravelly Run, Virginia, on March 31, 1865, for capturing nine Confederate soldiers and their flags. His Medal was not awarded until almost 52 years later on February 28, 1917, one of the last three Medals to be awarded for Civil War actions. He died on September 26, 1938, a month before his 94th birthday.

The last known surviving Union veteran (NOT a Medal recipient) was Albert Woolson of Minnesota who died on August 2, 1956, at the age of 109.

The last known surviving Confederate veteran is disputed because of missing or inaccurate Confederate records but the one most frequently listed is John Salling of Virginia who died on March 16, 1958, at the age of 112.

THE LAST KNOWN SURVIVING MEDAL RECIPIENT OF THE 1866-70 INTERIM PERIOD was Navy Seaman William Bradford Stacy. Born on March 4, 1838, he earned his Medal on January 15, 1866, for rescuing a shipmate from drowning. He died on May 3, 1921, at age 83.

THE LAST KNOWN SURVIVING MEDAL RECIPIENT OF THE INDIAN CAMPAIGNS was Army Private Allen Walker of Company C, 3rd U.S. Cavalry. Born on January 19, 1866, he earned his Medal on December 30, 1891, in Texas. He died on September 11, 1953, at age 87. The last known surviving veteran of the Indian Wars was Fredrak Fraske who died on June 18, 1973, at the age of 101.

THE LAST KNOWN SURVIVING MEDAL RECIPIENT OF THE 1871 KOREAN CAMPAIGN was Navy Landsman William F. Lukes. Born on February 19, 1847, he earned his Medal on June 9-10, 1871. He died on December 17, 1923, at age 76.

THE LAST KNOWN SURVIVING MEDAL RECIPIENT OF THE 1871-98 INTERIM PERIOD was Navy Gunner's Mate Third Class John Everetts. Born on August 25, 1873, he earned his Medal on February 11, 1898, for attempting to save a shipmate from drowning. He died on September 12, 1956, at age 83.

THE LAST KNOWN SURVIVING MEDAL RECIPIENT OF THE SPANISH-AMERICAN WAR was Navy Gunner's Mate Third Class John Davis. Born on October 28, 1877, he earned his Medal on May 11, 1898, while serving on the U.S.S. *Marblehead*. He died on June 9, 1970, at age 92. The last known surviving veteran of the Spanish-American War was Nathan E. Cook who died on September 10, 1992, at the age of 106.

THE LAST KNOWN SURVIVING MEDAL RECIPIENT OF THE PHILIPPINE INSURRECTION was Army Second Lieutenant John Thomas Kennedy. Born on July 22, 1885, he earned his Medal on July 4, 1909. He died on September 26, 1969, at age 84.

THE LAST KNOWN SURVIVING MEDAL RECIPIENT OF THE BOXER REBELLION was Navy Ordinary Seaman William Seach. Born on May 23, 1877, he earned his Medal on June 13-22, 1900. He died on October 24, 1978, at age 101.

THE LAST KNOWN SURVIVING MEDAL RECIPIENT OF THE 1899-1910 INTERIM PERIOD was Navy Fireman First Class Demetri Corahorgi. Born on January 3, 1880, he earned his Medal on January 25, 1905. He died on October 15, 1973, at age 93.

THE LAST KNOWN SURVIVING MEDAL RECIPIENT OF THE 1911 PHILIPPINE ACTIONS AGAINST OUTLAWS was Navy Carpenter's Mate Third Class Jacob Volz. Born on June 23, 1889, he earned his Medal on September 24, 1911. He died on July 22, 1965, at age 75.

THE LAST KNOWN SURVIVING MEDAL RECIPIENT OF THE VERA CRUZ MEXICAN CAMPAIGN was Navy Ensign George Maus Lowry. Born on October 27, 1889, he earned his Medal on April 21-22, 1914. He died on September 25, 1981, at age 91.

THE LAST KNOWN SURVIVING MEDAL RECIPIENT OF THE 1915 HAITIAN CAMPAIGN was Marine First Lieutenant Edward Albert Ostermann. Born on November 23, 1882, he earned his Medal on October 24, 1915. He died on May 18, 1969, at age 86.

THE LAST KNOWN SURVIVING MEDAL RECIPIENT OF THE 1915-16 INTERIM PERIOD was Navy machinist Charles H. Willey. Born on March 31, 1889, he earned his Medal on August 29, 1916. He died on September 11, 1977, at age 88.

THE LAST KNOWN SURVIVING MEDAL RECIPIENT OF THE DOMINICAN REPUBLIC CAMPAIGN was Marine First Sergeant Roswell Winans. Born on December 9, 1887, he earned his Medal on July 3, 1916, and later rose to the rank of Brigadier General. He died on April 7, 1968, at age 80.

THE LAST KNOWN SURVIVING MEDAL RECIPIENT OF THE 1919-20 HAITIAN CAMPAIGN was Marine Second Lieutenant Herman Henry Hanneken. Born June 23, 1893, he earned his Medal on October 31-November 1, 1919. He died on August 23, 1986, at age 93.

THE LAST KNOWN SURVIVING MEDAL RECIPIENT OF THE SECOND NICARAGUAN CAMPAIGN was Marine Corporal Donald Leroy Truesdell (name later changed to Truesdale). Born on August 8, 1906, he earned his Medal on April 24, 1932. He died on September 21, 1993, at age 87.

THE LAST KNOWN SURVIVING MEDAL RECIPIENT OF WORLD WAR I was Navy Lieutenant Edouard Victor Michel Izac. Born on December 18, 1889, he earned his Medal on May 21, 1918. Evidently a very hardy soul, Lt. Izac was captured when his ship was sunk by a German submarine. Enroute to a prison camp in Germany, he escaped by jumping through a window on a moving train. Recaptured, he escaped again, this time successfully, bringing back important information on German submarine movements. He died on January 18, 1990, one month after his 100th birthday.

THE LAST KNOWN SURVIVING MEDAL RECIPIENT OF THE 1920-40 INTERIM PERIOD was Navy Torpedoman First Class John Mihalowski. Born on August 12, 1910, he earned his Medal on May 23, 1939. He died on October 29, 1993, at age 83.

THE NUMBER OF LIVING MEDAL RECIPIENTS AS OF NOVEMBER 23, 2003, ARE:

World War II	50
Korea	18
Vietnam	64

Of the 132 living recipients, over half are retired from military service careers.

THE LAST AWARD FOR A NON-COMBAT ACTION was presented posthumously to Navy Boatswains Mate Second Class

Owen Hammerberg. He saved the lives of two fellow Navy divers while they were clearing wreckage in Pearl Harbor, Hawaii, on February 17, 1945. Pinned under the collapsed wreckage, Hammerberg survived for 18 hours before succumbing. This was also

THE LAST AWARD to date for actions inside the United States, its territories, possessions or protectorates.

BIBLIOGRAPHY

Ambrose, Stephen E., D-DAY, JUNE 6, 1944, THE CLIMAC-TIC BATTLE OF WORLD WAR II, Simon & Schuster, New York, NY, 1994.

Astor, Gerald, THE MIGHTY EIGHTH, Dell Books, New York, NY, 1997.

Benford, Timothy B., THE WORLD WAR II QUIZ AND FACT BOOK, VOLUME 2, Harper & Row, New York, NY, 1984.

Beyer, W.F., Edited by O.F. Keydel and, DEEDS OF VALOR, Platinum Press Inc., Woodbury, N.J., 1992

Black, Robert W., RANGERS IN KOREA, Ballantine Books, New York, NY, 1989.

Borthick, David and Jack Britton, MEDALS, MILITARY AND CIVILIAN OF THE UNITED STATES, MCN Press, Tulsa, OK, 1984.

Borts, Lawrence and Col. (Ret.) Frank Foster, U.S. MILITARY MEDALS, 1939 TO PRESENT, MOA Press, Fountain Inn, SC, 1994.

Bosiljevac, T.L., SEALS-UDT/SEAL OPERATIONS IN VIET-NAM, Ballantine Books, New York, NY, 1990.

Bowden, Mark, BLACK HAWK DOWN, New American Library, New York, NY, 1999.

Brokaw, Tom, THE GREATEST GENERATION, Random House, New York, NY, 1998.

Brunner, Borgna, Editor, THE TIME ALMANAC 2000, Family Education Company, Boston, MA, 1999.

Cebulash, Mel, MAN IN A GREEN BERET AND OTHER

MEDAL OF HONOR WINNERS, Scholastic Magazines Inc., New York, NY, 1969.

Clarke, John D., GALLANTRY MEDALS AND AWARDS OF THE WORLD, Haynes Publishing Group, Somerset, England, 1993.

Committee on Veterans Affairs, U.S. Senate, MEDAL OF HONOR RECIPIENTS 1863-1978, U.S. Government Printing Office, 1979.

DeLong, Kent, WAR HEROES, Praeger Publishers, Westport, Connecticut, 1993.

Donlon, Captain Roger, H.C., OUTPOST OF FREEDOM, Avon Books, New York, NY, 1965.

Garrison, Webb, CIVIL WAR TRIVIA AND FACT BOOK, Rutledge Hill Press, Nashville, TN, 1992.

Graham, Don, NO NAME ON THE BULLET, Viking Penguin Books, New York, N.Y. 1989.

Gurney, Gene, and Mark P. Friedlander Jr., FIVE DOWN AND GLORY, Ballantine Books, New York, N.Y., 1958.

Hirsch, Phil, Editor, FIGHTING ACES, Pyramid Books, New York, N.Y., 1965.

Hoyt, Edwin P., MCCAMPBELL'S HEROES, Avon Books New York, NY, 1983.

AIRBORNE, Stein and Day, Briarcliff Manor, NY, 1979.

Jason, Alexander, HEROES, The Anite Press, Pinole, California, 1979.

Johnson, Robert S. and Martin Caidin, THUNDERBOLT!, Ballantine Books, New York, NY, 1958.

Kaplan, Phillip and Rex Alan Smith, ONE LAST LOOK, Abbeville Press, New York, N.Y., 1983.

Lang, George, M.H., Raymond L. Collins and Gerard F. White, MEDAL OF HONOR RECIPIENTS 1863-1994, Facts on File Inc., New York, N.Y., 1995.

Lanning, Lt. Col. (Ret.) Michael Lee, THE AFRICAN-AMERI-CAN SOLDIER: FROM CRISPUS ATTUCKS TO COLIN POWELL, Carol Publishing Group, Secaucus, N.J. 1997

INSIDE THE LRRPS, RANGERS IN VIETNAM, Ballantine Books, New York, NY, 1988.

Manchester, William, AMERICAN CAESAR, Dell Publishing Co., New York, NY, 1978.

McCombs, Don and Fred L. Worth, WORLD WAR II SUPER FACTS, Warner Books Inc., New York, N.Y., 1983.

Moskin, J. Robert, THE U.S. MARINE CORPS STORY, McGraw-Hill Book Company, New York, New York, 1977, 1979, 1982.

Murphy, Edward F., HEROES OF WW II, Ballantine Books, New York, N.Y., 1990.

Norton, Major Bruce H., USMC (Ret.), ENCYCLOPEDIA OF AMERICAN WAR HEROES, Checkmark Books, New York, NY, 2002.

Phillips, William R., NIGHT OF THE SILVER STARS, Naval Institute Press, Annapolis, MD, 1997.

Plaster, John L., SOG: THE SECRET WARS OF AMERICA'S COMMANDOS IN VIETNAM, Simon & Schuster, New York, N.Y., 1997.

Rausa, Rosario, SKYRAIDER, Zebra Books, New York, NY, 1982.

Russ, Martin, LINE OF DEPARTURE:TARAWA, Zebra Books, New York,. NY, 1975.

Santoli, Al, LEADING THE WAY, Ballantine Books, New York, NY, 1993.

Shultz, Richard H. Jr., THE SECRET WAR AGAINST HANOI, HarperCollins, New York, NY, 1999.

Simpson, Charles M. III, INSIDE THE GREEN BERETS, THE FIRST THIRTY YEARS, Presidio Press, Novato, CA, 1983.

Stanton, Shelby L., GREEN BERETS AT WAR, Presidio Press, Novato, CA, 1985.

Tassin, Dr. Raymond J., DOUBLE WINNERS OF THE MEDAL OF HONOR, Daring Books, P. O. Box 526D, Canton, Ohio, 44701, 1986.

Walker, Dale L., LEGENDS AND LIES: GREAT MYSTERIES OF THE AMERICAN WEST, Tom Doherty Associates Inc., New York, N.Y., 1997.

Wallace, Irving, David Wallechinsky and Amy Wallace, SIGNIFICA, E.P. Dutton, Inc., New York, NY, 1983.

Warner, Ezra J., GENERALS IN BLUE; LIVES OF THE UNION COMMANDERS, Louisiana State University Press, Baton Rouge, Louisiana, 1964.

Westmoreland, General William C., A SOLDIER REPORTS, Dell Books, New York, NY, 1976.

Wright, Mike, WHAT THEY DIDN'T TEACH YOU ABOUT WORLD WAR II, Presidio Press, Novato, CA, 1998.

WHAT THEY DIDN'T TEACH YOU ABOUT THE AMERICAN REVOLUTION, Presidio Press, Novato, CA, 1999.

MAGAZINES AND JOURNALS:

Allen, Mel, PORTRAIT OF A HERO, Yankee Magazine, September, 1981.

ARMY DIGEST MAGAZINE, various issues.

BANNER, THE, a publication of the Sons of Veterans of the Civil War, Dunsmore Publishing, Scranton, PA, various issues.

Cortesi, Lawrence, TWO WHO DARED AT AP BAC, The American Legion Magazine, June, 1982.

Geere, Captain Marion, THE MEDAL OF HONOR, Gung Ho Magazine, August, 1982.

LIFE MAGAZINE, various issues.

Ross, H.L., SI PARKER_AND THE LAST SHALL BE THE FIRST, V.F.W. Magazine, April, 1974.

Schwartzberg, Richard, COL. GEORGE DAY, KEEPING WITH THE HIGHEST TRADITIONS, New Breed Magazine, June, 1982.

Smith, Larry, SOMETHING WORTH DEFENDING, Parade Magazine, July 2, 2000.

Snyder, James D., OUR MOST DECORATED SERVICEMEN, Parade Magazine, November 16, 1969.

Van Goethem, Larry, GIANTS OF THE CORPS, COLONEL JOSEPH J. MCCARTHY, Leatherneck Magazine, February, 1982.

Zumwalt, James, I WAS NOT GOING TO LET THEM DOWN, Parade Magazine, October 17, 1999.

NEWSPAPERS AND INTERNET WEBSITES:

The Daily Oklahoman
The New York Daily News
The New York Post
The New York Times
The Congressional Medal of Honor Society:cmohs.org
U.S. Army Center of Military History
DefenseLink: U.S. Department of Defense
Fourchaplains.org
Homeofheroes.com
Medalofhonor.com

About the Author
RON OWENS

After serving more than 30 years with the Oklahoma City Police Department, Ron Owens retired as a Captain commanding the Criminal Intelligence and Gang Enforcement Units. A native son of Oklahoma City and a graduate of the University of Central Oklahoma, Owens spent his first 18 years on the force as a Patrolman and Detective including 8 years in Homicide, 11 years as a Hostage Negotiator on the Tactical Team and other assignments in Narcotics, Sex Crimes and Special Projects. As a Lieutenant, he was one of the two instructors for the OCPD's first official training course for investigating Officer-Involved Shootings.

Mr. Owens has published three previous books focusing on law enforcement history. He currently lives in Oklahoma City, Oklahoma.

Now he turns his focus upon his military brethren and the recipients of the nation's highest military honor for combat heroism, the Medal of Honor. This book is a tribute to their valor.

Other Books by Ron Owens

Jelly Bryce: Legendary Lawman
Oklahoma Heroes
Oklahoma Justice

Printed in the USA
CPSIA information can be obtained
at www.ICGtesting.com
JSHW082158140824
68134JS00014B/312